FREE TO BE DIFFERENT

Other titles in the London lectures series published by Marshalls

The Year 2000 AD. *ed. John Stott*

Free To Be Different

Varieties of Human Behaviour

Malcolm Jeeves
R. J. Berry
David Atkinson

Marshalls

Marshalls Paperbacks
Marshall Morgan & Scott
3 Beggarwood Lane, Basingstoke, Hants., UK.

First published by Marshall Morgan & Scott 1984

ISBN: 0 551 01122 X

Phototypeset by Input Typesetting Ltd, London
Printed in Great Britain by Camelot Press Ltd., Southampton

Contents

Foreword

The longing for freedom has been one of the features of the post-war world. Although its most violent and widespread eruption was in the 1960s, it has continued to simmer ever since. The campaign for human rights and for racial and sexual equality, the quest for a more equitable economic order that would eliminate poverty and hunger, the environmental debate and the peace movement, not to mention the various liberation theologies, are all signs and symptoms of the same craving to be free. Yes, and free to be different. In spite of the natural tendency to conform to our own peer group and subculture, there is a horror of enforced stereotypes. We detest totalitarian regimes that permit neither dissidents nor deviants. A so-called freedom that results in drab uniformity is a contradiction in terms. It is also an affront to our human dignity. We yearn for freedom because we sense that this is what it means to be a human being. We should be free. We could be free. Indeed, we *are* free, for we are responsible moral agents, capable of making our own choices and decisions.

Yet much in the modern world is signalling a different message. Millions of people are suffering from political or economic oppression or both. The 'alienation' of the worker from the fruits and rewards of his labour, of which Marx wrote, has become a general sense of social powerlessness. Ordinary citizens feel themselves victims of a situation over which they have no control. They sense they are *not* free to be different. On the contrary, the forces of the technocracy threaten to crush all personal individuality out of them. Then along come scientific scholars who philosophise their plight for them. They neither are, nor have been, nor ever could be free, they are told. For in reality human beings are 'nothing but animals' driven by instinct, or 'nothing but machines' programmed to make automatic responses to external stimuli.

Against this reductionism, or 'nothing buttery' (to use an expression first coined, I think, by Professor Viktor Frankl in *From Death*

Camp to Existentialism. 1959, but popularised by Professor Donald MacKay), the 1982 London Lectures made a vigorous protest. They were delivered by a psychologist (Professor Malcolm Jeeves), a geneticist (Professor Sam Berry) and a theologian (Dr David Atkinson), from St Andrew's, London and Oxford Universities respectively. The three lecturers accept that both our genetic inheritance and our social environment exercise strong influences upon us, but they deny that 'we are nothing more than our genes', that the mechanisms of the brain rule out freedom of choice, or that we are merely the product of environmental conditioning. So this book, which contains the revised lectures, is an interdisciplinary rejection of determinism and an assertion of human responsibility. The three lecturers are also at one in being Christians. Each is struggling to integrate his expertise not only with the disciplines of the other two, but also with his own biblical faith.

The result is a fascinating investigation into the respective influences on human behaviour of 'nature' (our genetic inheritance), 'nurture' (our social conditioning) and 'grace' (God's loving and transforming initiative). In addition to a lecture on each of these three topics, three case studies are developed, relating to religion, sex and conscience, and to the bewildering variety of religious, sexual and moral (or immoral) practices in which human beings indulge. What is the origin of all this diversity? Does it supply evidence of freedom or of determinism?

All three lecturers keep returning to Jesus Christ. For it is he who offers us unconditional acceptance. He also calls us to be different from the world around us and from what we ourselves once were. He endows us with gifts that equip us for different tasks and enrich our common life by their very diversity. He provides an authentic norm by which to evaluate alternative expressions of belief and behaviour. Above all, he sets us free, not by granting us a freedom without limits (limitless liberty is an illusion) but by enabling us to be the unique person he created and intends us to be. We find ourselves only by losing ourselves in the service of God and others.

John R. W. Stott,
Chairman of the London Lectures Committee and
Director of the London Institute for Contemporary Christianity.

The Lecturers

R. J. (Sam) Berry D.Sc., F.R.S.E., is Professor of Genetics and teaches in the Department of Zoology at University College, London. He is President of the Linnean Society, Chairman of the Research Scientists' Christian Fellowship, and a council member of the Natural Environment Research Council. He is also a lay member of the Church of England's General Synod and of its Board for Social Responsibility. Besides scientific papers, he has written a number of books, including *Teach Yourself Genetics, Adam and the Ape, Inheritance and Natural History,* and *Neo-Darwinism.*

Malcolm Jeeves is Vice-Principal of St Andrew's University, Professor and Head of its Department of Psychology, and a Fellow of the Royal Society of Edinburgh. Having researched and taught at both Cambridge and Harvard, he was for a number of years Professor of Psychology at the University of Adelaide, South Australia, before going in 1969 to St Andrew's. His main research interests are in neuropsychology and cognitive science. He is the author of several books including, *Analysis of Structural Learning* (with G. B. Greer), *Experimental Psychology: An Introduction for Biologists, Thinking in Structures* (with Z. P. Dienes), *The Scientific Enterprise and Christian Faith* and *Psychology and Christianity – The View Both Ways.*

David Atkinson is Chaplain of Corpus Christi College and Member of the Faculty of Theology in the University of Oxford. He is also a visiting lecturer at Wycliffe Hall, Oxford, and Theological Consultant to 'Care & Counsel'. He obtained his Ph.D. in Organic Chemistry at King's College, London, and an M.Litt. at Bristol University. Following his ordination, and curacies in Bolton and Birmingham, he became Librarian of Latimer House, the Anglican Evangelical Research Centre in Oxford. His books *Homosexuals in the Christian Fellowship* and *To Have and To Hold* (on marriage and divorce) have won wide acclaim for their theological insight and pastoral sensitivity.

Note The London Lectures in Contemporary Christianity were founded in 1974. Their purpose is to develop biblical Christian thinking on the issues of the day. They are delivered annually, in association with the London Institute for Contemporary Christianity, which is now located in St Peter's Church, Vere Street, London W1. Neither the Council of the London Institute nor the London Lectures Committee necessarily endorses all the views that the lecturers express.

PART I INFLUENCES UPON US

1: Environmental conditioning

Malcolm Jeeves

Since freedom of choice is such a common feature of our everyday experience, one may ask why this book should have the title *Free to be Different?* There are a number of reasons.

First, some argue that our experience of freedom is illusory and our actions are predetermined. In support, they point to accumulating knowledge in the biological and behavioural sciences that, they say, reveals more and more how limited our real freedom of choice is. Did we but know it, they contend, the combined effects of our genetic inheritance, the upbringing that we received and the social group within which we live have, to all intents and purposes, determined the sort of people we have become and shall become.

Secondly, we discover on reflection not only that all of us all the time make implicit assumptions about our own freedom and about other people's freedom, but that such assumptions affect our own behaviour and, equally important, shape our attitudes and actions towards those around us. In other words, attribution of the roots of actions in ourselves and others have consequences for social action. Thus, the assessment we make of the differences we observe between individuals and groups has implications for how we behave towards those who differ from us whether as individuals or as groups.

Thirdly, if the different beliefs we hold can all be traced to predetermining influences, then surely, it is argued, this supports a form of relativism that says, in effect, that any one belief is as good or bad as any other.

Fourthly, the suggestion that the whole story about the determinants of behaviour can be told, in principle at least, by biological and behavioural scientists, runs counter to the Christian belief –

and indeed experience – of the gracious activity of God in the lives of men and women.

Running through the reasons just listed are a number of issues that we shall discuss in this book. I shall devote the remainder of this chapter to examining whether, or to what extent, the experience of freedom is an illusion. This in turn will involve a detailed consideration of some of the determinants of behaviour. I shall also be asking what follows from the findings that I review. What attitudes does it call upon us to take towards ourselves and others? In Chapter 4 I shall examine the differences we observe in religious beliefs, practices and behaviour. I shall ask how these come about and whether they imply a necessary relativism in evaluating beliefs.

Professor Berry will examine the evidence for genetic determinants of individual differences of character and behaviour and ask what implications this has for a Christian assessment of freedom. Dr Atkinson will take up the question how the gracious activity of God sustains and changes behaviour and beliefs.

Preliminary considerations

Determinism

Determinism is not a new problem thought up by psychologists in this century. It has been a perennial one for philosophers, scientists and theologians. Without doubt, however, the rapid growth of the biological and behavioural sciences in the last two centuries has given encouragement to the determinist presuppositions of some philosophers and psychologists. This, of course, is not a problem for Christians only. All who believe that human beings have choice and carry responsibility must grapple with it.

On the one hand, common experience tells us that the reality of freedom of choice is not to be laid aside because of a passing fashion in psychological theorising, whether it be Skinner or Freud. To sweep under the carpet the most immediate evidence we have of daily experience would be unscientific indeed. On the other hand, we are all aware of the extent to which the sort of people we are, the things we say and do, and the aspirations we hold are a very complex amalgam of factors, including our genetic inheritance, our early upbringing and school environment, and the wider social milieu in which we have lived. Problems then remain. What are the limits to our freedom of thought and action? Are we as free to change as we have imagined? No one comes to these problems without presuppositions. What are the presuppositions most likely to be held by behavioural scientists?

Psychologists accept the need to assume some form of determinism in order to make their work meaningful. At its simplest, the psychologist believes that what he does one day under one set of conditions will be reproducible another day under the same set of conditions. Some take the view that what would happen on both occasions would be precisely the same (this is sometimes referred to as 'strong determinism'); others that on the two occasions the outcome would be similar within close statistical limits ('weak determinism'). Thus, in common with other biologists, psychologists have a working assumption of some degree of determinism; they assume that even the most complicated forms of behaviour should ultimately be capable of description in mechanistic terms. Another way of expressing this is to say that we find it useful to adopt a 'what if' kind of approach in our model-building and theorising. This approach can lead us astray only if, for example, we progress unthinkingly from asking 'what if' man's psychological processes are like those of a complex computer, to asserting that therefore man is nothing but a complex machine. Certainly, from the Christian point of view, there is nothing at stake in recognising that in scientific research something may be gained by developing and testing a variety of models of man. But such research benefits do not necessarily lead to the conclusion that man is nothing but each of the models we develop. That a deterministic and mechanistic approach to the study of behaviour brings research benefit, is amply borne out by the success achieved so far. Most working biologists are, in fact, methodological determinists. At the same time, few psychologists or biologists doubt the reality of their own freedom of action or that of their colleagues. If they did, they would be moving away from methodological determinism to metaphysical determinism. And indeed, within the history of psychology this century, a number of notable figures have written as if they were metaphysical as well as methodological determinists. The two most noteworthy are Freud in the first half of the century and, in the last thirty years, Professor B. F. Skinner of Harvard.

Since in the minds of many people the terms psychology and psychoanalysis have become synonymous, this demands, if for no other reason, that we spend a little time considering Sigmund Freud's views of determinism. One of the important features of his theory was to stress the effect of happenings in the early life of the individual upon later development and behaviour. He was convinced that factors of which we are frequently unaware and which often occurred in our early years largely determine our thought and behaviour at any moment. Perhaps Freud's most lasting contribution is his emphasis on the unconscious and its continuing effects on our behaviour. It is curious that psychoanalytic theory, while it has been seriously criticised and often rejected by academic psychologists, nevertheless still grips and fascinates the man in the street. One of the fairest assessments of Freud that I have come across was made by Professor George Miller. Some years ago he wrote, 'Freud struggled to see man as he is, not as he ought to be or as Freud would have liked to imagine him.' He went on: 'after he [Freud] had completed his demonstration of the importance of the unconscious instinctual forces in human conduct, the old faith in the inevitability of human progress through man's constant growth in knowledge and understanding sounded like an innocent myth concocted to amuse little children'.[1]

The contrast with the other arch-determinist among the psychologists of this century could hardly be more striking. Whereas Freud depended almost entirely upon the reports of his subjects and their introspections, and then upon making assumptions about their private mental life, Skinner will have none of this. Starting from the fact that all forms of behaviour have consequences, he has systematically studied the ways in which by manipulating them, behaviour can be shaped, established or got rid of. Writers in this field, following the terminology introduced by Skinner, regard the most influential shapers of behaviour as of two kinds. These are 'reinforcers', known to us more familiarly as rewards for action, and 'punishers', consequences that are unpleasant in one way or another. As a result of many years of sustained laboratory work, Skinner has increased our understanding of how reinforcers and punishers shape and control behaviour, whether of animals or of humans. The behaviour-shaping techniques arising out of Skinner's work are in wide use today, in order to train complicated patterns of behaviour as well as simple skills. For example, retarded and psychotic patients in hospital wards have been helped by the use of his methods. The key notion behind all Skinner's work is thus that behaviour is shaped and maintained by its consequences. In Skinner's own words, 'What all of this and that complicated verbiage means is that we are studying the ways in which the consequences of behaviour are contingent upon what an organism is doing in a given situation'[2].

In his later thinking and writing, Skinner has described his belief that techniques of behaviour modification can be harnessed to shape the future of our society. These views are summarised in his book *Beyond Freedom and Dignity*.[3] Since in his view behaviour in every society is constantly being shaped and controlled, the question arises as to who should do the shaping and controlling. More simply, who shall control the controllers? Are the controllers to be scientists? If so, what if the scientists differ among themselves about the ideal goals to which society is to be directed? It is clear from what Skinner writes in *Beyond Freedom and Dignity* that for him cultural relativism is the order of the day. Thus, he writes, 'What a given group of people call good is a fact; it is what members of the group find reinforcing as a result of their genetic endowment and the natural and social contingencies to which they have been exposed. Each culture has its own set of goods, and what is good in one culture may not be good in another.' Another American psychologist, Dr O. Hobart Mowrer, raised the obvious question, 'suppose the scientists exercising control differ among themselves on what is good for the masses?' There seems little escape from the conclusion that Skinner is a metaphysical reductionist and not merely a methodological one. Thus, when pressed to explain why he was not committing the error of reductionism, he readily agreed that the mechanics of, for example, how a person comes to know God (which is a proper topic for the scientific study of religion) could not possibly on logical grounds refute the reality of the God believed in by the man who was being studied. Dr Willard Day, reviewing Skinner's book in *Contemporary Psychology*, echoes a similar judgment: 'the book simply does not deal with issues that threaten in the least what people are actually doing when they concentrate their lives on the activities they regard as robustly meaningful in a spiritual or even religious sense'.[4]

Before leaving Skinner, we must point out that those who accept his views discover on further reflection that they have strange implications. For instance, does his view of freedom mean that he had no freedom to arrive at any view other than the one he arrived at? According to his own formulation of the controlling factors in behaviour, his verbalisation of his views was no more than the determinate outcome of the schedules of reinforcement to which his life events had exposed him over the years. Are there then no external criteria for deciding whether or not Skinner himself is right or wrong? Indeed, are words like right and wrong, true and untrue, meaningless words in his view? I think the dilemma into which such a thoroughgoing determinism leads one was best summed up in a slightly different context by the late Professor J. B. S. Haldane when commenting on deterministic views of brain functioning. He wrote, 'If my mental processes are determined wholly by the motions of the atoms in my brain, I have no reason to suppose that my beliefs are true, and hence I have no reason for supposing my brain to be composed of atoms'.[5]

This dilemma is also acknowledged by Professor Carl Rogers, a distinguished and well-known contemporary psychotherapist. He accepts that whilst it is proper for the behavioural scientist to assume prior causation in the determination of behaviour, nevertheless responsible personal choice is the core experience of psychotherapy.

Indeterminacy and Complementarity

We have seen that working psychologists adopt a strategy of methodological determinism, but that the extent to which this becomes a metaphysical determinism varies between one psychologist and another. Even the leaders in neuro-science do not all believe that because the brain may be studied as a determinate system, the mind is therefore similarly determinate in its action. Furthermore, to pretend that any current theory is the last word and is going to remain totally unchanged, is to be unaware of the accelerating pace of research in neuroscience. Those who wish to adhere to the possibility of an indeterminate brain structure can remain in excellent company, no less than that of two recent Nobel prizewinners. Sir John Eccles, the physiologist, certainly takes an interactionist view of the mind and brain that claims indeterminism. More recently, Dr Roger Sperry of California, who was awarded the Nobel Prize in Medicine, takes a similar view, though the basis for his beliefs are slightly different. Along with the approximately 0.1 per cent mentalist minority, he supports a hypothetical brain model in which consciousness, and mental forces generally, are recognised as important features of the control.[6]

Others working in neuroscience do not see it as necessary to assume a physically indeterminate brain in order to safeguard the possibility of freedom of choice. For example, Professor Donald Mackay, who delivered the 1977 London Lectures, denies that the assumption of a physically determinate brain structure precludes the possibility of freedom of choice. He argues for what he calls the logical indeterminacy of freedom of choice.[7]

It must be acknowledged, therefore, that in the field of determinism and its relation to freedom of choice and action there is a wide range of opinion. On the one hand, there are those who regard the evidence as not strong enough to lead to the assumption of a physically determinate brain. On the other hand, there are those like MacKay who take the view that to regard the brain as a physically determinate system is a good working assumption, but add that this does not exclude the possibility of freedom of choice and action. Clearly, the physical working of the brain is an issue that will go on being discussed for many centuries yet.

What is of more immediate concern to us, is that the evidence that environmental factors shape and constrain behaviour is already sufficiently compelling to make it essential for Christians to examine its implications and to identify the appropriate attitudes that we should have towards ourselves and others in the light of it. Before doing this, however, there is another commonly held presupposition among biological and behavioural scientists that we must examine. Most psychologists consider it futile to regard the explanations that they formulate at one level as being necessarily in competition with explanations given at other levels. Every piece of behaviour is so complex that any hope of gaining a full understanding of its causal roots invites study at several different levels, for example, the biological, the stimulus-response, the cognitive and the social. When it comes to deciding which level of explanation is the most appropriate for a particular problem, one may well find different psychologists holding different views. It is now not scientific data that influence the decision, but rather the personal philosophies, research strategies and hopes of the scientists concerned. Some, today I think a minority, believe that the ultimate goal of all explanation is to reduce everything to what they regard as the most fundamental level possible, such as the subatomic one. Others take the view that the level of explanation invoked must be appropriate to, and do justice to, the nature and complexity of the behaviour being studied.

The notion that there are several levels of explanation, or a hierarchy of explanations, in which psychology would perhaps appear below anthropology and sociology, but above physiology, genetics and biochemistry, is a familiar one. The attempt to expand the terms of reference of physiology so as to embrace psychology is as much to expand physiology as to reduce psychology – a point not always apparent to some thoroughgoing reductionists. Whether science is to be unified by proceeding upwards or downwards through this hypothetical hierarchy remains an open question. Most psychologists, however, make the tacit assumption that their primary concern is the behaviour of the whole organism. To do this is not to deny the importance or relevance of a particular level of explanation, on which we may concentrate as we study behaviour in a particular situation, but rather to acknowledge that all levels are necessary if we are ultimately to do justice to the full complexity of human behaviour.

A question remains, however. If different explanations of the same set of events, offered by psychologists as well as sociologists or physiologists, are not to be regarded as competitors, then how are they to be related? Are there no limits to the number of explanations that we must accept? Are there any criteria for helping us to decide whether two explanations are complementary or competitive? As MacKay has pointed out on several occasions, before explanations at different levels can properly be seen as rivals, it needs to be shown that they are not in fact complementary. This is important, because what applies to the relation between these scientific explanations also applies to the task of relating religious and psychological accounts of behaviour. In each case, it is essential to realise that proof of complementarity does not establish that each account is true.

What we are saying, then, is that it is mistaken on both logical and empirical grounds to assert that psychology (or for that matter biology) leads inevitably to reductionism. Accounts of behaviour that are given in terms that assume personal responsibility for actions and beliefs, are neither valueless nor irrelevant. To say that they are would be as illogical as saying that a 'fasten your seatbelt' sign in an aeroplane is nothing but wires and bulbs and that you may therefore ignore it; or that the words addressed to you by a friend are nothing but sounds analysable without remainder on a sound spectrograph, so that you may ignore them; or, to come nearer home, that in this lecture all that is happening is that a hundred and fifty four pounds of wobbling protoplasm are emitting sounds of a certain wavelength. That is no doubt true, but I trust that in addition a message is being communicated to you. It is empirically evident that questions about, for example, personal relations cannot be properly formulated, let alone answered, by referring purely to physiological mechanisms. The choice of one approach, which may in itself be extremely productive and lead to important discoveries, may at the same time exclude even the formulation, at a different level, of equally important questions about the same event.

Failure to grasp this simple but basic point has been at the root of a good deal of meaningless and fruitless debate in recent years, both within psychology and between psychology and other disciplines. The necessity of studying behaviour simultaneously from several standpoints, in order to do justice to its complexity, does not mean that every explanation is acceptable, however fanciful. Each must be justified as necessary to a full understanding of what is being studied, and each must bring forward evidence relevant to the level being advocated.

With this necessary ground-clearing behind us, we may now move on to consider why psychologists believe there is accumulating evidence for the view that our behaviour is to a considerable extent shaped and moulded even 'determined', (remembering the caveats I have already entered) by earlier as well as contemporary events. In so doing, we shall be looking at different levels of explanation from the biochemical and physiological to the psychological and possibly sociological.

For the convenience of exposition, we shall consider the determinants from two points of view, which I will call the 'bottom-up' and the 'top-down' approaches. By the bottom-up approach I refer to the attempt to trace the springs of our behaviour and the source of individual differences to factors such as genetic loading, and the early environment both physical and social. By the top-down approach, I refer to the shaping (if you like 'conditioning') effect, self-initiated or received, of the ideas, beliefs, goals and aspirations of individuals and groups.

Determinants of behaviour

The bottom-up approach

Let us consider some examples of the environmental determinants of behaviour, beginning with the earliest pre- and post-natal physical determinants. Since this is tantamount to saying 'let us review psychology', you will realise that I am being extremely selective and merely choosing examples to make a general point. Determinants of this kind do not start at birth, but are often pre-natal. This is still after the genetic blueprint, of which Professor Berry writes in the next chapter, has been laid down. I give only one example of such a determinant, which can be either pre-natal or post-natal or both. I refer to the effect of nutritional factors on later development. To deprive an organism of food for any length of time produces a sharp drop in body weight, whereas in the adult brain weight remains relatively unimpaired. The body, it would seem, sacrifices every other organ to protect the brain. In infancy, however, the story is different. Work on animals has shown that if neonates are malnourished or undernourished during times when normally there is rapid brain growth, not only will body weight be dramatically affected but the growth of the brain will be retarded. The evidence from such studies appears to show that even if the animal is subsequently to eat as much food as it can, brain growth may never catch up.

While it is difficult to summarise in a few words the results of human researches on malnutrition, it is fair to say that nearly all the studies reported over the last twenty years have supported the view that it can cause cognitive impairment. Memory, it would seem, is least impaired, and early language impairment decreases with age, but certain spatial and perceptual skills show a consistently large impairment. It is possible, however, that the impairments observed in reasoning and conceptual ability may not be attributable simply to malnutrition but also to the cumulative effects of a generally deprived and non-stimulating environment. One encouraging note to emerge is that where social and nutritional deprivation has been permanently alleviated, a reversal of the earlier cognitive impairments has occurred.

Another example of the effect of early environment on development comes from the work done in California by Professor Mark Rosenzweig and his colleagues. They studied matched litter mates of rats, half of which were allowed to grow up in large cages with what were called 'toys' to play with, while the other half were brought up in cages on their own. All had the same amount of food, drink, daylight and so on. It was discovered, however, that at adulthood those that had been brought up in the enriched environment with 'toys' showed much more rapid learning ability in typical maze-learning situations and, perhaps more importantly for our purposes, their brain weight was significantly greater than in those brought up with as much food and drink as they wished, but in the socially impoverished environment. Moreover, the chemical activity in the brains of the enriched animals was shown to be significantly different from that of the impoverished animals.[8] This, of course, raises the question as to what extent such findings apply unbeknown to us in the human condition.

Although the effects of malnutrition on the development of the brain are certainly a serious problem, they are in a sense predictable. More surprising are the results of studies of the effects of brief sources of stimulation on organisms during infancy. For example, it has been shown that mild sources of stress such as handling for a few minutes, which occur in critical periods during infancy, can have profound effects on subsequent behaviour, effects that seem to be out of all proportion to the magnitude of the events themselves.[9]

When put into situations that provoke fear and anxiety, the animals handled during infancy showed much less fear and more rapid learning. Most studies of this kind, as well as those by Rosenzweig and his colleagues, generate problems for the experimental psychologist. For example, the long-term consequences of the deprivations described by Rosenzweig are still not clear, since it would appear that some of the changes, at least those related to the biochemical amino acid levels, can be reversed by functional stimulation even after prolonged deprivation in the early life of these animals.[10] The parallel with the human situation is difficult to draw, but perhaps we should note that where children come from impoverished environments, they are likely to suffer both nutritional and environmental deprivation, and therefore the effects we have noted may be compounded.

Continuing our consideration of the effects of early environment on later behaviour, we come to what has now become the classic study by Professor Harry Harlow. He showed that when baby monkeys are reared without their mothers or without adequate surrogate mothers, they may fail to develop normal social relationships when they mature. Of particular interest in Harlow's work was the discovery that it is the touching, the physical contact rather than the suckling, that is important for the development of normal affectional behaviour. Having said this, we must again immediately enter a caveat. We should not conclude that the social behaviour of an organism is determined entirely by experiences occurring during the first weeks or months of life. We shall return to this in a moment when considering the work of Dr John Bowlby and of Professor Jack Tizard.

Anyone who has read the excellent book *Early Experience: Myth and Evidence*[11] will know what a conceptual minefield one enters when trying to disentangle the seemingly conflicting strands of evidence. The authors point out in their concluding chapter that there is today a 'received wisdom' that says that the first few years of life are of vital long-term importance. So strongly is this view held, they believe, that it becomes reinforced by selective perception and clinical experience.

In the first place, as Professor Urie Bronfenbrenner has shown,[12] studies of pre-school intervention, almost without exception, show substantial IQ and other cognitive gains during the programmes. If the programme finishes, however, there is a progressive deceleration in IQ so that after four years they are back to base line. Where IQ increments are apparent three or four years after intervention has ended, it seems attributable not to the programme *per se*, but to a more enduring change in parent-child interaction.

Turning now from intellectual development to social and emotional competence, how do early life experiences affect us? The most widely publicised findings, in recent years, have come from studies of the effects of institutional rearing. Studies of children who grow up in good, well-equipped and well-staffed modern institutions have tended to show that the undesirable outcomes of such institutionalisation (emphasised in earlier studies) need not be as enduring as the much publicised views of Bowlby had implied.[13] Nevertheless, they still demonstrate the adverse effects of some kinds of early experience. For example, although the institutional children studied by Tizard from 1974 to 1978 showed an ability to catch up with the controls on cognitive and language tests, they nevertheless showed more enduring rather diffuse behavioural changes best exemplified by the way in which they all the time sought to gain attention. At school these differences became more marked. They were, to quote a recent summary by Dr Michael Rutter, 'more attention seeking, more restless, disobedient and unpopular'.[14]

Despite all the research done so far, the Clarkes maintain that 'as yet there is no clearly developed comprehensive model of how the physical and social environment affects children during the course of growth.'[15] Having said that, some balancing comments are called for. The Clarkes also conclude: 'Moreover, it does not seem any more promising to think in terms of critical events: apart from those which make it impossible to sustain life, it appears that there is initially no psycho-social adversity to which some children have not been subjected, yet later recovered, granted a radical change of circumstances.'[16] They further comment that 'What emerges very strongly from our evidence is the need for a greater recognition of the possibility of personal change following misfortune.'[17] This is not to deny that in some cases constitutional factors may set an upper limit to such improvements.

More positively, the Clarkes point out that the whole of development is important, not merely the early years. To accept as final some of the current over-simple notions may result in self-fulfilling prophecies. Of those, more in a moment.

Much attention has been paid in recent years to the effects on individuals and groups of attitudes and policies towards racial groups. For example, studies in predominantly white countries have shown a generalised effect on the self-esteem of young black children. When black children are put into experimental situations that are claimed to measure their self-esteem, it is found that they show markedly lower self-esteem than appropriately matched groups of white children. Such effects, it would seem, persist: adults in small ethnic communities are reported to show a self-esteem and self-evaluation lower than that for matched samples of white adults.

In this brief consideration of the effects of social environment, it is perhaps worth commenting on the possible effect that schooling may have upon achievement and intelligence. A number of studies appear to demonstrate the effect of a self-fulfilling prophecy such as I mentioned above. Studies of this kind use a system whereby a teacher or parent is given an expectation of a child, and it is then found that this expectation will actually mould the child's progress so that the child fulfils the prophecy set for it. In one study, for example, teachers were led to believe that some of the children had scored high on a 'test for intellectual blooming'.[18] The children's actual level of ability was measured before and after their interaction with the teacher, and the self-fulfilling prophecy was indeed found to be operating. This, I am told, is typical of many studies. They demonstrate how a socio-cultural definition of a person's position, or even an interpersonal impression of another person, if maintained consistently, may have a long-lasting effect on the child or adult, thus enhancing any already existing individual differences.

The top-down approach

If my reading of the writings of social psychologists in recent years is correct, there has been an enormous increase in a different kind of research. Its results emphasise the importance of a person's convictions about his personal freedom for the self-determination of his own behaviour. This research has to do with what is called the 'locus of control' of behaviour. Although the concept of a person's locus of control is not without ambiguity, a large number of studies have shown that people differ, often widely, in their assessment of the measure of control they think they have on their environment. They also differ in how they feel about such control.

Professor David Myers[19] has recently pointed to the extensive research literature which explores the consequences of people's belief that they control their own destiny as opposed to assuming that their fate is beyond their control.

One frequently quoted study by J. Rodin and E. J. Langer[20] will serve to illustrate this point. They began by suggesting that one of the reasons for the debilitated condition of many elderly people living in institutions was their perception of having no control. The residents of a nursing home were, in their study, randomly assigned to one of two groups. One group was briefed by the staff in a way which stressed the staff's responsibilities for them and their activities. The other group was given instructions that maximised the residents' sense of their own control. The results were striking, in view of the slight differences in instructions. Those in the group in which personal control had been stressed reported significant increases in personal happiness three weeks later. The nurses' and physicians' judgments matched the subjects' own reports. Eighteen months later, the effect was still evident. Most striking of all, whereas 30 per cent of the low responsibility group had died, the corresponding figure for the responsible group was 15 per cent.

Myers generalised these findings into a speculation, namely that the psychological teaching given in colleges over the past two decades, about the very strong effects of environmental control, has led to an increased sense of powerlessness among many growing young people. If they believe that the forces that constrain their development are all important, then understandably they may feel powerless to do anything about such forces. One much publicised set of researches in this area is subsumed under the label of 'learned helplessness'.

The leading researcher in this field, Martin Seligman,[21] defines it thus: 'When a person is faced with an outcome that is independent of his responses, he *learns* that the outcome *is* independent of his responses.'

In a typical study, animals discover that their own behaviour cannot provide an escape from slight electric shocks. Such animals later fail to take any initiative in other situations when in fact they *could* escape and avoid punishment. By contrast, animals which are taught personal control by successfully escaping any first shocks they are given are found to adapt easily to a new situation. Seligman has pointed to similarities with human situations, such as when depressed or oppressed people become passive about their situation because they believe that whatever they do, their actions can make no difference. Findings in this area of research, on subjects ranging from helpless dogs to residents of institutions, thus confirm *the extreme consequences of losing one's sense of personal control over the environment*. A recent critical review by C. B. Wortman and J. W. Brehm[22] makes it clear that caution is needed in interpreting the results of human studies of learned helplessness. They write, 'Most of the studies that report helplessness effects have methodological problems, or plausible alternative explanations'[23] While this debate will continue, however, the point of it for us is that what a person believes about his freedom to control his life has important consequences for his behaviour, health and well-being.

We may quote one further example from the literature on locus of control which is related to research on so-called need-achievement. For more than twenty five years, social psychologists have pursued research into the differences between those individuals who seem to be attracted by tasks which require skill and pose a challenge to do something well – (the so-called 'high achievers') and those who seem threatened by failure and thus avoid activities where their performance may be evaluated (the so-called 'low achievers'). Recent studies have shown how belief about locus of control interacts with this variable of need-achievement. It appears that people judged to have high need-achievement, who also believe that they have internal locus of control, are optimistic and outgoing. By contrast, those who have an equally high level of need-achievement, but who are convinced that the external locus of control is an all-important factor in their lives, soon slide into a state of despair.

Those working in this field see these studies as offering strong remedies. In looking at ourselves and understanding ourselves, we should realise the importance of our beliefs about our personal freedom, and remember that we tend to become what we imagine ourselves to be. Freedom is not just a matter of pressures upon us, but also of our own internal beliefs. As Myers has put it, 'people who believe they have response-ability act with more responsibility.'[24] This surely echoes the scriptural injunction given from Genesis onwards that man is called upon to have dominion over the creation, which includes himself. Should he not then begin by recognising his divinely given internal locus of control and seek to have dominion over himself? Certainly, in Scripture, we are encouraged not to let the world squeeze us into its mould, but rather be transformed by the internal renewing of our minds (Rom. 12.1, 2).

Some conclusions

The examples I have reviewed point towards two distinguishable lines in contemporary psychological research.

On the one hand, there are the demonstrable effects of the physical and social environment in shaping our behaviour and setting limits to our capacities. On the other hand, there is the accumulating evidence that highlights the crucial importance for our well-being and our behaviour of how we see ourselves and our relation to our environment. These two emphases, I suggest, are complementary, not conflicting, for each is true and valid. Both are necessary in order to do justice to the total evidence. What implications do they have, then, for a sober assessment of ourselves? And how do they look in the light of what God has taught us about ourselves and this world?

First, all of us all the time make implicit assumptions about our own freedom and about other people's freedom. Such assumptions lead to actions. Lest the current state of knowledge of the physical and social determinants of behaviour be overstated, it is salutary to remember that in practice we psychologists do not do very well in predicting or controlling the behaviour of either individuals or groups. The unaccounted-for variance in our data, the 'error' factor in our results, remains uncomfortably large. In practical terms too, our attempts at, for example, the rehabilitation of persistent offenders, still leaves a great deal to be desired. Were we as successful in controlling and manipulating the determinants of behaviour as some would have you believe, we should be much better placed to offer solutions to some of our more pressing social problems.

The importance of having as detailed an understanding as possible of the environmental forces at work is that we may hope from such understanding to improve our schools, homes, churches and other familiar social institutions.

Secondly, what may be an appropriate strategy for the psychologist to adopt in his research may be an entirely inappropriate one to adopt as his dominant self-image. Here is the importance of the complementary emphasis. The studies of locus control confirm what we have long known, but been in danger of forgetting, namely that how we see ourselves in relation to others and to our environment has far-reaching consequences for the sort of people we become.

If the appropriate attitude to adopt towards ourselves is to give primacy to the exercise of our personal freedom, it is sad to reflect upon how seldom we in fact do so. Instead, we readily blame the environment for our failures, while taking credit for our successes. But this goes back a very long way. Adam, you will remember, attributed responsibility elsewhere: 'the woman you put here with me', he said to God 'she gave me some fruit from the tree, and I ate it' (Gen. 3.12) (NIV).

When considering what is the appropriate attitude to adopt to others, there is wisdom in accentuating the research I reviewed earlier, which showed that people are significantly determined by their social, environmental and cultural conditioning. The environmental determinants of behaviour are more extensive than many people realise or are willing to accept. A full recognition of the weight of environmental conditioning does, I believe, lead to a greater likelihood of adopting Christian attitudes and actions towards others. For these are more likely to follow from the assumption that their behaviour is determined, than from the belief that they are totally free to do whatever they wish, whenever they wish. Social behaviour, it is clear, is more dependent upon the specific situation within which a person finds himself than upon general personal dispositions. The more we appreciate this, the less vulnerable we shall be to social manipulation. It is more typical of us, however, to see it the other way round. We too readily err in attributing causality. What I am suggesting is that in trying to understand a causative effect on a person's behaviour, we should adopt a dynamic model that sees a reciprocal causation between persons and environments. On the one hand, this would be in contrast to an entirely one-sided mechanistic, behaviouristic model such as would be taken by a thoroughgoing follower of Skinner. On the other hand, it would be different from the view taken by someone who believed that the individual is the sole determinant of his personal decisions and initiatives. Neither extreme, I suggest, represents the truth of the situation, which is that each of us has real freedom of choice, although within limits that vary from individual to individual and from situation to situation. For the Christian, this conclusion needs qualifying because, as Dr Atkinson will make clear, the grace of God gives us ground to stand on in order to be responsible. God's grace enables us to make a realistic assessment of ourselves, and at the same time it becomes a resource, strengthening us to live differently in full awareness of our limits.

To sum up then, it would be appropriate from a Christian point of view, and also consonant with contemporary psychological research, to hold complementary views of ourselves and of others. We should regard ourselves as responsible agents for our own actions, but think of others as being determined to a considerable extent by their environment. Such a view would, among other things, have the effect of cultivating within us the practical fruits of self-discipline and self-initiative, while recognising the forces that press upon our friends and colleagues. I invite you to consider whether this is not in fact the emphasis of Scripture. When addressing us directly, the Bible emphasises our responsibility for our own failings. However, when talking to us about others, whether it be the poor or the disadvantaged, it frequently advocates the complementary perspective that we should act with compassion towards them, that we should take the beam out of our own eye before worrying about the splinters in others'. Indeed, it would encourage us to let judgment begin at the house of the Lord. Sadly, we often reverse this wisdom. We excuse our own failures, but attribute personal responsibility to the poor for their slothfulness, despite the fact that their plight may be largely determined by environmental circumstances.

I conclude, therefore, that taking full cognisance of the weight of contemporary psychological evidence, there remains ample room for a clear concept of human freedom within a deterministic science. Recent research strengthens our awareness of human freedom. At the same time, it is well to remember that we so often underestimate the extent to which others are externally controlled and in so doing, we too easily develop our own self-serving attitudes of prejudice and pride.

For Christians, however, our ultimate hope and confidence lie not in making ourselves acceptable to ourselves, with excuses based on the effects of environmental forces, but upon the gracious unconditional acceptance of our Creator. Our conviction is that no human being has any ground on which to stand except God's grace. So that is where we stand. Here alone our true liberty is to be found.

Notes

1. G. A. Miller, *Psychology: The Science of Mental Life* (Hutchinson, London, 1964) p. 244

2. B. F. Skinner, in *Firing Line,* a transcript of a programme dated 17 October 1971, p. 6
3. B. F. Skinner, *Beyond Freedom and Dignity* (New York, 1971; Jonathan Cape, London, 1972)
4. W. Day, *Contemporary Psychology,* Vol. 17, September 1972, No. 9, pp. 465–468
5. Quoted in J. N. D. Anderson, *Morality, Law and Grace* (Tyndale Press, London 1972)
6. R. W. Sperry, *Bulletin of the Atomic Scientists,* Vol. 22, No. 7, 1966, pp. 2–6
7. D. M. MacKay, *Human Science and Human Dignity* (Hodder and Stoughton, London, 1979)
8. M. R. Rosenzweig, et al, *Chemical and Anatomical Plasticity of Brain,* Science, Vol. 146, No. 3644, pp. 601–619, 1964
9. S. Levine, *Science,* 1967, 1156, pp. 258–260
10. S. P. R. Rose, *The Conscious Brain* (Weidenfeld and Nicholson, 1972)
11. Ann M. Clarke and A. D. B. Clarke, *Early Experience: Myth and Evidence* (Open Books, London, 1976)
12. op. cit. Chapter 14
13. J. Bowlby, *Maternal Care and Mental Health* (Geneva: World Health Organisation, 1951)
14. M. Rutter, Parent-Child Separation: Psychological effects on the children, Chapter 10 in *Early Experience,* op. cit.
15. ibid. p. 265
16. ibid. p. 268
17. ibid. p. 271
18. R. Rosenthal and L. Jacobson, *Pygmalion in the Classroom* (Holt, New York, 1968)
19. D. G. Myers, *The Human Puzzle* (Harper and Row, New York, London, 1978), p. 235
20. E. J. Langer and J. Rodin, The effects of choice and enhanced personal responsibility for the aged: A field experiment in an institutional setting. *Journal of Personality and Social Psychology,* 34, 191–198, 1976. J. Rodin and E. J. Langer, Long-term effects of a control-relevant intervention with the institutionalized aged. *Journal of Personality and Social Psychology,* 35, 897–902, 1977)
21. M. E. P. Seligman, *Helplessness: On depression, development and death* (W. H. Freeman, San Francisco, 1975)
22. C. B. Wortman and J. W. Brehm, chapter in *Advances in Experimental Social Psychology* (Academic Press, 1975), pp. 277–336
23. ibid. p. 306
24. *op. cit.* p. 242

2: Genes and responsibility

R. J. Berry

The Bible is absolutely clear that every human being is unique and knowable by God as an individual. Christ spoke in the parables of the sower and of the talents about everyone having different gifts (Matt. 13.23; 25.15), and both Paul and Peter emphasise the need to use our own particular gifts if we are to fulfil the role that God has for us (Rom. 12.6; 1 Cor. 7.7; 12.4–11; 1 Pet. 4.10,11; etc.). God recognises and cares for each one of us personally, and not merely because we are members of a category as his children or those who acknowledge him (John 10.3, etc.).

Running alongside this teaching on divinely provided uniqueness is the dominant theme in Scripture that we are all alike created, redeemed and sanctified by God's sovereign grace, and that there is no possibility of living the life God has purposed for us except through his way. All our Christian teaching emphasises the need for personal regeneration and spiritual growth, and stresses the impossibility of achieving these unless we pass through the one 'narrow gate'.

This leads to the idea that there exists such a thing as a *normal* Christian life: conformity is identified with sound doctrine and any deviation is heresy. There is a public image of a Christian as a uniform subfusc – drear, earnest in conversation and conservative in habit. This image is changing, partly on theological grounds[1] and partly on sociological ones (changes in worship patterns, etc.), but there is no real challenge to the simple concept of a Christian ideal. After all, we are all descended in sin from a single Adam (Rom. 5.12), or at least a single pair, and we are all called to be 'like Christ' (2 Cor. 3.18), which gives little opportunity for variety.

How then do we reconcile the immensity of human variation with the call to live in conformity to the divine image? When Paul tells us that 'There is neither Jew nor Greek, slave nor free, male nor female, for you are all one in Christ Jesus' (Gal. 3.28) (NIV), does this mean that we are to eliminate our differences, and that failure to do so is sin? Put bluntly, are all differences between human beings the result of the Fall and therefore eradicable by grace, or is human variety God-given so that its suppression is wrong? Sexual difference antedates the Fall, and is described by God as being 'very good' (Gen. 1.27, 31; 2.20–3), but a traditional interpretation of the Tower of Babel story (Gen. 11.1–9) is that racial and linguistic differences date from the Babel fiasco; in other words, mankind was culturally homogeneous until that post-Fall event.

The implicit tendency among Christians, therefore, is to regard differences between individuals as unfortunate and sinful. Since redeemed mankind will all come together in the same place (Isa. 49.22; Rev. 21.24–6; etc.), it follows that grace will overrule such differences, and that their manifestation in any person shows a lack of sanctification. Individual variety must, it is argued, be subjugated to the true goal of Christlikeness (1 John 3.2).

In contrast, the trend in secular Western societies is to emphasise the importance and power of individual traits. To live a full life, a person must express his individuality. In particular, if his (or her) personal idiosyncrasies are inherited, he is applauded for building on them, and excused from moral blame if they are antisocial (even if some expressions of personality have to be restrained for the good of society). Liberal culture has its problems here: although it is prepared to allow and encourage musicians to be musicians, mathematicians to be mathematicians, and homosexuals to be homosexuals, even it draws back from permitting the aggressive to be muggers or kleptomaniacs to be licensed robbers.

This complex set of attitudes to individual variety shows a clear difference between Christians and non-Christians, and confusion in secular society about the extent to which individual desires should be cultivated. In Chapter 1 Malcolm Jeeves has shown how some of our personal foibles are produced by differences in our upbringing, and he develops this theme in Chapter 4 where he considers the source and maintenance of some of our religious differences. This chapter is concerned with the extent and meaning of inherited differences between individuals, and in particular whether they determine or limit our options and opportunities in life. Are we prisoners of our genes? Do the genes we inherit from our parents excuse our weaknesses or explain our superiority? How much of our behaviour and fate is under the control of our environment (which can be changed), and how much of it was fixed when a sperm and an ovum met nine months before our birth and developed into the person we are? The consequent question about the role of divine influences in moulding the set of gene-environment interactions that make up each one of us is explored by David Atkinson in Chapter 3.

Genes and gene action

Each one of us has twenty-three chromosomes supplied by our father, and twenty-three by our mother. If the fusion between two particular paternal and maternal gametes had not occurred, we would not exist. Those forty-six threads of a simple and chemically understood complex between protein and deoxyribonucleic acid (DNA) are the ultimate biological basis of each of us. It is wholly incorrect, however, to claim that the 'genetic code' of the 20,000 or so genes on the forty-six chromosomes gives a complete or adequate specification of the human being that develops from the fusion of egg and sperm. We need to recognise at least three complicating factors:

Genetics and epigenetics

The DNA of the chromosomes is 'translated' into chains of amino acids (polypeptide chains), which in turn form into proteins and enzymes. But the production of polypeptide chains is not an automatic production process that goes on throughout life. Genes are subject to a precise control or regulation, with many (indeed, most) being switched off most of the time. The genes in every cell in the body are affected by the history and environment of that cell, and the bulk of the chromosome set which is replicated in most body cells is non-functional. Cells in which this control process breaks down are liable (if they survive) to be cancer-producing.

However, the development and functioning of a whole organism is even more complicated. Some of the proteins that are the primary gene products are recognisable in a normal body; they turn up as enzymes controlling vital processes or antigens affecting particular immunological reactions. The products of most genes interact together in the body to form secondary compounds, which are building blocks for growth and maintenance, hormones, and so on. These interactions are highly complex and specific; in no way can the human body be regarded as the simple consequence of a set of random chemical specifications. Although virtually all our characters can be regarded as affected by genes, their inheritance should be described as *epigenetic* rather than genetic; in other words, it is the result of processes acting subsequently to the primary action of the genes themselves.

Genes and environment

The primary gene products are the direct consequence of a rather simple chemical process that has been worked out in the revolution of molecular biology that began in 1953 with James Watson and Francis Crick's elucidation of the structure of DNA. At this level, inherited characters can be said to be determined by the genes carried by an individual. Once we leave the primary gene product level, however, the occurrence, speed and direction of the chemical processes in the body are affected to varying extents by environmental influences. This is of considerable importance in clinical medicine, because inherited defects in metabolism can often be corrected once they have been identified. For example, diabetes can be treated with insulin, haemophilia with anti-haemophilic globulin, phenylketonuria and galactosaemia by withholding from the diet phenylalanine and galactose respectively. It is not true that genetic disease cannot be treated, as used to be believed.

The interaction of genes and environment applies throughout normal development. Pre-natal growth is slowed by the mother smoking, and maternal drinking may reduce the intelligence and size of a baby at birth ('foetal alcohol syndrome'). Childhood growth can be affected by nutrition. IQ is higher in first children, and in small families than in larger ones.

It is often difficult to work out the details of gene-environment interactions in humans where experimental breeding and environmental control cannot be carried out. Comparison of the behaviour and achievements of identical and non-identical twins, and of adopted and natural children, can go some way to understanding these processes, but the available data are very limited. Criminality and sexual deviation have often been attributed to childhood or to inherited influences but, as we shall see in Chapter 5, the grounds for distinguishing between these are usually equivocal. Notwithstanding, there can be no doubt at all that we are affected as radically by our environments as by our genes.

Although identical twins (that is, genetically identical individuals) are often strikingly alike in both behaviour and physical traits even when reared apart, nevertheless there are plenty of examples where identical twin pairs show marked and significant differences for some characters. Our genes cannot express themselves in a vacuum; even in cases where our genes predispose us towards certain characters (as a shallow hip-joint to congenital hip dislocation or an extra Y chromosome pushes us in the direction of mindless aggression), there is no *automatic* association between gene and the physical or behavioural trait that finally emerges.

Foetal death

The third complication is different. So far we have considered the complex relation between genes and characters. There is also a non-simple relationship between the fertilised egg and survival to adult life. For every 100 eggs subject to normal internal fertilisation, 85 will be fertilised if intercourse is frequent, 69 are implanted, 42 are alive one week later, 37 at the sixth week of gestation, and 31 at birth. Between a third and a half of the foetuses that spontaneously abort in the first few weeks of pregnancy have an abnormal chromosomal complement (97 per cent of babies with a single sex chromosome (Turner's syndrome) and 65–70 per cent of Down's syndrome (mongolism) have miscarried by the eighteenth week). It seems likely that a large proportion of those with central nervous system anomalies (anencephaly, spina bifida, etc.) are spontaneously aborted and so survival to birth is not the norm; it occurs in only a minority of conceptuses, and many of those eliminated are recognisably abnormal in their genetic complement.

When we consider together interactions between genes, interactions between genes and the environment, and foetal death, it is obvious that we are determined by our genes only in a very loose sense. Some of the differences between us are the result of different genetic complements, but these differences can be magnified or diminished by family, social, educational, cultural, or other environmental influences. Even someone whose hereditary make-up irrevocably fixes some traits – such as a person with Down's syndrome – nevertheless can show a wide range of behavioural responses from gross mental defect to approaching normality. Although in one sense we must be regarded as the sum of the genes we acquired at conception, in another sense we are considerably more than that sum. The wetness of water cannot be predicted from the atomic properties of its constituent hydrogen and oxygen, and human beings cannot adequately be described by their genes, even if we could know the details of all the DNA of an individual.

The genetic control of behaviour has been much discussed in recent years, particularly since the publication of Edward Wilson's *Sociobiology: The New Synthesis.*[2] Some of the claims and arguments that this has inspired are reviewed in Chapter 5. For the moment all that is necessary is to note that few behavioural traits are irrevocably determined by genes; virtually all human behaviour (and associated characters, like intelligence) can be unintentionally or consciously influenced by the environment. Although it is true that behaviour is inherited, it is equally true and perhaps more helpful to recognise that there is no gene for any behaviour.

Man – the image of God

We are biological machines. But Christians believe that we are also spiritual beings, made in the image of God. This is not to say that we are simply biology plus spirit, but that we ought, properly, to understand ourselves as a unity. The difficulty is that a biologist could describe all the genetic, embryological and obstetrical processes that lead to the formation of an individual, and not need to refer to God once. Is there then room for a soul? Or is 'man made in the image of God' wishful thinking? Medieval scholars capitalised on biological ignorance, and sited the soul in an organ that did not appear to have any useful physical function. The pineal gland was a favourite location.

A few years ago, Christians tended to fit God into the apparent gaps in determinacy revealed by modern physics; Heisenberg's uncertainty principle was much quoted in this context. If it is theoretically impossible to predict the exact position of an electron at any one time, it follows (so it was argued) that God could control physical events at the most fundamental level and hence remain sovereign in an apparently mechanistic universe. John Hick has tried to apply such ideas to molecular biology. He sees our soul as represented by the 'genuine element of unpredictable contingency', and our 'uniqueness' as residing in our genes.[3] In other words, God uses the combinatorial process of gamete formation to ensure our freedom.

Such reasoning has been attacked by Donald MacKay on many occasions.[4] He sees attempts to find physical holes into which to put God as simple extensions of the 'God of the gaps' mentality that has bedevilled theologians ever since the rise of modern science, and that has resulted in God being relegated to the ever-shrinking areas of ignorance. J. B. Phillips popularised the fallacy of this thinking by his phrase 'your God is too small'[5] and its prevalence was amply demonstrated by the response to John Robinson's *Honest to God*[6] which showed how much people still think of God as a benign old despot living above the bright blue sky.

The children's idea of God as a merciful tyrant, which was exposed by J. B. Phillips and John Robinson, is not far removed from the idea of a divine manipulator squeezed into the holes of a causal scientific network. In contrast, and following a very distinguished tradition extending at least as far back as Aristotle, and including philosophers all down the ages,[7] MacKay has argued that the answers provided by science can only be a proportion of those that arise with relation to any event or process. For example, a picture can be described in terms of the distribution and chemistry of the pigments that make it up; it is possible to give a complete mechanistic explanation in this way. But it can also be described in artistic terms, dwelling upon its composition and use of colour, and the intention of the artist in painting it as he did. The two descriptions do not overlap in any way; both are complete in themselves. MacKay sees our understanding of God and his work as *complementary* to that of science, in exactly the same way as the chemical and artistic descriptions of a picture are *complementary*. He has developed this approach to show that human free will is retained even if brain processes are completely known.

Michael Polanyi has used a different argument, which leads to the same conclusion. In *Knowing and Being*[8] he points out that all machines (physical or biological) restrict nature in order to work, and that these restrictions in practice impose 'boundary conditions' on the laws of physics and chemistry. These boundary conditions link processes of different levels; Polanyi regards the functioning of a whole organism and the chemistry of the DNA from which it comes as being different levels. The rules applying to different levels are different. In the complementarity example used above, the explanations in terms of physics and chemistry, and in terms of purpose and design, are on different levels and hence are subject to different understandings.

It is easy to dismiss the ways that MacKay and Polanyi approach living organisms as playing with words, but they are both concerned with the extremely important principle that scientific knowledge is limited by questions frameable in scientific language. Do the answers to important questions depend on nothing more than our ability to formulate them? Or are there really different levels to our being that exist, however philosophers or scientists address them? We must beware lest we assume that a problem does not exist because we have an answer to part of it, or fail to take into account all the factors that may bear on it.

The Bible uses a variety of different expressions to describe man's nature. These all describe different aspects of our whole: physical, social, emotional, spiritual, etc. So far I have tended to speak of man as having a spiritual element in his being. Colloquially, this tends to be referred to as the possession of a soul. Can we recognise this? A previous generation of theologians tended to equate the possession of a soul with rationality. There is certainly no scriptural support for that: rather, as Karl Barth has pointed out,[9] man is not just an animal endowed with reason, but 'is the subject of history which has its ground in God's revelation to us', and thus differs from the animals. Man alone is faced by God, and has to make responsible decisions before him. Emil Brunner[10] is even less anatomical, insisting that God's image in us is to be understood as a reflection. He refers to 2 Corinthians 3.18: 'We all, with unveiled face reflecting as a mirror the glory of the Lord, are transformed into the same image from glory to glory'. He concludes: 'Man's meaning and his intrinsic worth do not reside in himself but in the One who stands "over against" him, Christ the Primal Image, the Word of God.' Hence man's 'distinctiveness is not based upon the power of his muscles or the acuteness of his sense-organs, but upon the fact that he participates in the life of God, God's thought and God's will, through the Word of God'. There have been many other ideas put forward about the nature of 'image'. A helpful contribution is that of C. F. D. Moule[11] who describes the situation in a positive way, 'The most satisfying of the many interpretations, both ancient and modern, of the meaning of the image of God in man is that which sees it as basically responsibility' (Eccls. 17.1–4). Perhaps the best recent summary is that of H. D. MacDonald,[12] who proposes that 'image' should be taken as indicating 'sonship', which holds together both the ontological and the relational aspects of the image. Responsibility is thus the obedience of a son to God his father, exemplified perfectly in Jesus.

The unanimous conclusion, therefore, from biology, philosophy and theology is that God's image in man is a relationship initiated by God and hence dependent upon his sovereignty. It is inaccurate to think of it as some physical connection between God and man's body: this is not suggested by Scripture, nor supported by any of the arguments summarised above. God created both life and man, and they are 'good', but we must not assume on these grounds that they are materially identifiable or intrinsically protected. For the status of life in God's eyes we must examine other evidence.

Life – and death

A proper understanding of God's image as explored in the previous section is fundamental to any useful discussion of the relation between body and soul, and to linking our knowledge of biological life and its variation with God's influence on us and the effects of the Fall.

The first thing to recognise is that we are wholly man-souls; we are not simply animals with divine essence added (and, by implication, with the possibility of it being subtracted). This is not the place to develop this theological point, which is firmly based in Scripture, but it is important, in view of our later discussion of biological life, to underline that we are unitary beings, and that the idea that the soul is the essential reality and can be distinguished from the body, is derived wholly from the Greek Platonist tradition.

But having said this, we must remind ourselves that the creation of man is described in the Bible as a two-stage process: the physical form was made by God and *then* he 'breathed into his nostrils the breath of life, and man became a living being' (Gen. 2.7) (NIV). As Calvin wrote, man is linked with the natural creation by his body being made of the same substance as the rest of creation, and distinguished through being 'endued with a soul, whence it received vital motion; and on this soul God engraved his own image, to which immortality is annexed'.

The distinctiveness of the specially human part of this creation is clearly shown by the Bible's description of the effects of the Fall, when Adam and Eve were excluded from God's presence and introduced death into the world, and that death 'reigned from Adam' (Rom. 5.12–14). It is important to note, however, that *physically* Adam and Eve lived on and produced a family. There is a tendency to speak of the Fall as having 'marred' or 'obscured' God's image, and that it can be restored in Christ. But there can be no disagreement that our physical existence has carried on since the Fall despite the fact that unredeemed mankind has been 'dead in trespasses and sins' since then, and the Scripture is explicit that the spiritual Fall (involving disobedience to God) has interacted with the biological realm to produce recognisable symptoms (Gen. 3.14–19; Rom. 8.20–4). In some sense, biological and spiritual life can be distinguished from each other, although we must be careful not to over-emphasise this possibility since they are part of a whole.

What are the essential properties of biological life? Here we can be simple. Although living systems are very complicated, the two features that characterise all of them are replication and mutation – the capacity for like producing like, and the capacity for change.[13] Other properties that we associate with life, such as complexity, response to outside stimuli, or interactions within and between organisms, are all secondary to these two basic attributes. Life depends on replication and mutation, and these in turn can be understood by our knowledge of DNA and the genetic code. I have already stated (p. 38), 'in principle a biologist could describe all the genetic, embryological, and obstetrical processes which lead to the formation of an individual, and not need to refer to God once'. But since then we have seen that the omission of God in such a description does not in any way imply either a denial of his existence or any assumption that he is not involved in the processes.

Which brings us at last to the crucial question: how should we use our knowledge of God to view human diversity, and make ethical judgments on the manipulation of life?

We can recognise four principles in our discussions so far:

1. God has a special relationship with man, distinct from that of animals. Christians were prominent in forming animal welfare societies, on the grounds that we have a responsibility to care for the whole creation. But current arguments of animal welfare activists are based on assuming that all animals are equal and that 'lower' animals need protection from bullying by man; this has led ironically to a denial of the Christian position.[14] God has created all life and committed its care to us (Gen.1.26), but there is little in principle different from our dominion over and responsibility for (say) a stretch of spectacular sea cliffs or a fertile valley on the one hand and a population of unique bacteria, cockroaches or rats on the other. Biological existence *per se* must be respected, but is not subjected to any special protection in the Bible.

2. The death that came into the world at the time of the Fall was spiritual death, separation from God. The time of the Fall is a matter of dispute, but even those who assert that the Creation and Fall took place over a very few days a few thousand years ago have to face the fact that plant death at least must have taken place before the Fall (and the death of a plant is biologically no different from that of an animal); while those who take the more orthodox view that life on earth existed many millions of years before man appeared and fell are faced with death (and extinction) on a very large scale.[15]

3. A living organism is more than the product of its genes. This is especially true of man, who we accept by faith[16] as having a wholeness because he is made in God's image.

4. We do not develop in a vacuum. Both our physical being and our behaviour are shaped by interaction between genes and environment. It is not accurate to speak of genes as being 'bad' or 'deleterious', but only to recognise that a characteristic may be harmful *in a particular environment*. Short-sightedness is a problem to a hunter, but can be repaired by spectacles; aggressiveness may be a problem in an urban, sedentary environment, but may have been necessary to survival in a less regulated society. It is easy to multiply such examples: the point to emphasise is that our genetical

makeup is not *per se* all-determining. Rather, the person forged from those genes as he has passed through pre-natal environment, childhood and ultimately maturity, is inseparable from his history. The danger before all of us is failing to attain maturity because we have not exercised our ability to choose our environment (and by 'choosing our environment' I include the possibility of seeking or rejecting social, intellectual and spiritual milieux).

The role of fusion of male and female gametes in forming new human potential was not recognised until the seventeenth century; the cell basis of this was not described until the end of the nineteenth century. To the Bible writers (and for many centuries after them) 'life' was a great mystery. *Cogito ergo sum* was as near as secular man could get to describing it. We can now describe physical life in great detail. Some laboratory experiments have come close to making 'new' life. It is now possible to understand the molecular biology of human reproduction in great detail. It can be argued that life is continuous: gametogenesis, fertilisation, embryogenesis, birth, growth, reproduction, fertilisation, can be divided into recognisable periods, but the divisions are arbitrary. The gametes are just as unique as the fertilised ovum; the embryo is unable to live independently[17] of its mother for at least four or five months after fertilisation (and nowadays that stage is more dependent on medical technology than on biology); and so on. The situation is that we can speak perfectly correctly of a developing baby as either 'a miracle of new life' and/or as merely 'another manifestation of continuing human existence'. We are using different language for the same reality (or describing 'different levels') when we do this. It is particularly important to recognise this distinction when we are speaking about 'life'. For sometimes we are referring only to 'biological' processes, but at other times to 'human' life in the biblical sense of 'made in the image of God'. The latter is sacred, while the former is worthy of respect but not inviolable.

Ethical problems

Christians have a bad reputation for failing to test the implication of new facts in the light of Scripture. Copernicus and Galileo were persecuted for suggesting that the earth moved round the sun because this contradicted the current interpretation of the statement in the Psalms, 'the world is established; it shall never be moved' (93.1) (RSV). In early modern times the Church argued against closing in sewers, because these could be used by God to bring plagues upon sinners. It is obviously necessary to ask whether the knowledge about life that has come from our better understanding of biology has any effect on our attitude as Christians to the manipulation of life, ranging from artificial insemination to 'mercy killing'. This exploration of all relevant information is a very different procedure from the avowedly reductionist approach of Jacques Monod[18] or Robin Holliday,[19] who regard life as only a physicochemical system. It should also be distinguished from the theological approach of Joseph Fletcher[20] who interprets Scripture in the light of science rather than attempting what we are doing here, which is to test whether our interpretation of the Bible is correct as our knowledge of God's 'Book of Nature' increases.

A cynic may complain that looking again at traditional interpretations is the first stage in bowing to secular pressures. Indeed, many Christians insist that ethics are God-given, and therefore absolute and unchangeable. Certainly God's moral will does not change. Nevertheless, each new generation has to struggle to understand his revelation and to apply it to the questions of the day. We may conclude that previous interpretations were right, or we may decide that they may need revision. There is nothing immoral about examining our presuppositions: Christ himself set the pattern in the Sermon on the Mount, where six times he contrasted the teaching of the Pharisees ('you have heard it') with his own interpretations. The Pharisees may or may not have been deliberately distorting the law. In either case their understanding was incorrect. We must beware lest we too are over-dogmatic regarding the ethics we think we derive directly from Scripture.

The questioning is particularly pertinent for anyone familiar with the complexities of the arguments and counter-arguments about the nature of life or of sex, or the relationship between marriage and reproduction. When arguments become complicated, we need to ask if they have the right basis. Again we must look to Christ's example. William Temple, in commenting on John 4.19,20, points out that 'as so often with our Lord's reply to enquirers, he does not answer the question, but leads to ground where the question does not arise at all. It is often so. There is no Christian solution of the problems presented by human self-will; but there is a Christian cure for the self-will, and if that is effective, the problem is not solved but abolished'.[21]

The discussion of ethical problems that follows is not intended to be a blind reappraisal of accepted attitudes, but an exploration of alternative ways of looking at old problems. My suggestions may be right or wrong, but the way they should be tested is by Scripture, not by tradition or dogma.

Artificial insemination

Attitudes to artificial insemination, particularly by donor (AID) as opposed to by husband (AIH), have changed radically over the past few years: an Anglican report in 1948 condemned the practice; Pope Pius XII denounced it as immoral and absolutely unlawful; a Home Office report in 1960 believed that AID 'falls within the category of actions known to students of jurisprudence as liberties which, while not prohibited by law, will nevertheless receive no support or encouragement from the law'. By 1981 Gordon Dunstan[22] was able to summarise the situation more analytically:

> The ethics of AIH are uncomplicated – except for persons with objections to masturbation *per se* – and are those normal to such medical investigation and intervention. The ethics of AID are more complicated: for the spouses, in relation to their perception of marriage; for the practitioner in his part in a transaction still, in most jurisdictions, unrecognised by law and which results in a child of uncertain identity and status.

We are not concerned in the present context with the legal status of children born from artificial insemination. The key question concerns the morality of a third person coming into a marriage relationship. It has sometimes been argued that a woman commits adultery by accepting sperm from a man who is not her husband. This is not so, however. Marriage in the Bible was created primarily for social reasons and not merely for sexual relations ('It is not good that the man should be alone' (Gen. 2.18 (AV)); we must beware lest we interpret the phrase 'one flesh' as simply indicating physical coupling, when the Bible usage of 'flesh' refers to much more than our biological body (Ps. 16.9; Prov. 14.30; 2 Cor. 7.5; Col. 2.1; etc.). Christ's view of adultery (Matt. 5.27,28) goes beyond the legal definition of sexual intercourse (which requires some degree of penetration of the female organ by the male organ). Scripture uses two words to describe the physical union of a man and a woman, conveying a deep sense of the emotional and spiritual aspects of our sexuality. The first word is *kollaō* – to join, glue or cement together; its strengthened form *proskollaō* as found in Matt. 19.5 – 'a man shall . . . be joined to his wife and the two shall become one flesh'(RSV). The second word is *ginōskō* – to know. It is used only twice in the New Testament in the sense of physical union (Matt. 1.25; Luke 1.34). These two words bespeak the very deep emotional and spiritual relationship between a man and a woman, the physical vehicle and sign of which is sexual intercourse.

Being joined with another in marriage does not depend on the procreative aspect of sexual intercourse and, therefore, AID of itself does not infringe such a relationship between a man and his wife nor produce it between a woman and the donor. It is, of course, possible that AID carried out for the wrong motives could infringe Christ's high view of sexual purity. Under these circumstances it would be wrong and ought to be readily recognised as such.

Dunstan has pointed out that condemnations of AID concentrate on 'the violation of nature and the breaking of the ordained nexus between sexual love, procreation and family life. In substance these arguments are consequential, and can be put to the test of experience and empirical proof'. Such tests have only just begun to be made, largely because the whole artificial insemination procedure is surrounded, for understandable reasons, by secrecy. Snowden and Mitchell[23] believe that this secrecy 'is undermining the social values of openness, honesty and truthfulness on which social institutions and the institutional behaviour we know as family life rests'. They call for some statutory regulation of the practice. Notwithstanding, a Swedish study of couples who had produced children by AID reported an almost universal satisfaction and enrichment of their marriage as a result of it,[24] while only four out of fifty Australian couples reported any problems, all with the husband's attitude to the child.[25]

Artificial insemination is a remedy for childlessness. A question that has to be faced by every childless couple is whether they might not be able to fulfil themselves more and serve the community better if they were free of children. Paul certainly suggested this in his much maligned strictures about marriage (1 Cor. 7.32–5). A recent Free Church Federal Council and British Council of Churches' working party examined *Choices in Childlessness*[26] but came up with no invariable recommendations.

In vitro *fertilisation*

The possibility of 'test-tube' fertilisation raises spectres of an engineered Brave New World. But the ethical issues raised by *in vitro* fertilisation (IVF) *sensu stricto* are no different from those in AID. Indeed, if the semen comes from the husband and the ovum from the wife, the procedure is in principle the same as AIH.

However, IVF means that developing embryos are susceptible to study and manipulation outside the body; what are the limits to this? And, more emotively, are investigations on early human embryos tampering with God's own prerogatives in relation to man?

The two principles we must keep before us are the need to 'play safe', so that we are certain we do not maltreat human life, and the recognition that biological life is not the same thing as human life. A hydatidiform mole or a million sperm can be thrown away with little qualm, but what is the status of a fertilised ovum? Gordon Dunstan[27] has proposed what he calls a 'rebuttable statement of principle':

> One term used by moralists in moral analysis is the *finis operis:* the end or purpose to which an action or a function is ordered. Thus, the *finis* or end of spermatogenesis is the fertilisation of the ovum; the end of ovulation is the same; the two ends are complementary, towards the further end of producing live progeny. When these ends are frustrated by pathological impairment, research and experimental practice directed toward enabling the end to be achieved are *prima facie* licit (all the accepted ethics of consent, risk, etc. are assumed to obtain). Further, since the end of procreation is to produce healthy, viable progeny, research and clinical experiment directed towards the detection and elimination of disabling defects are also *prima facie* licit. The statement echoes the language both of natural law ethics and of consequential or utilitarian ethics. It does not imply that any end may be pursued regardless of means. In human procre-

ation, the concept of humanity may itself impose moral restraints upon the choice of means and also determine the moral worth of ends.

The right way forward (albeit tentative) at the moment would seem to be to acknowledge God's sovereignty over all life; to acknowledge that his image in us places a definite limitation on the extent to which we may manipulate human material; but at the same time to acknowledge that he expects us to use the skills we are given for proper ends, such as research on the causes of malformation and handicap. Only if we take an absolutist position like that of Paul Ramsey,[28] who demands that any procedure must involve no risk whatsoever to an unconsenting child, can we decide differently.

Cloning

The artificial production of multiple copies of the same genetic complement, by using adult cells (more strictly, the *nuclei* of non-reproductive cells) as egg cells has now been achieved in mice. A detailed account of the process in man has been given by David Rorvik *In His Image*[29] although this is now acknowledged to be fictional. Such cloning is a favourite science fiction scare story (Aldous Huxley's *Brave New World* depended on it).

Cloning seems unlikely ever to become commonplace, even if it becomes technically possible. But without reviewing all its advantages (such as eliminating the manifestation of genetic defects) or disadvantages, on the basis of the argument developed in this chapter, it is clear that a cloned individual would be just as much a creature in God's image as is an identical twin. Problems specific to cloning (additional to those in IVF, etc.) only arise if God 'comes in' to development at a particular stage.

Abortion

The possibly artificial problem of the time that God 'comes in' to development leads naturally to the question of abortion. Objection to abortion is almost entirely based on the fact that a developing embryo is inevitably 'en-souled' or, as Protestants might rather say, a 'complete person'. But what does this mean? That God stamps himself on an embryo at the moment sperm and ovum fuse? Does this mean when the first cell division takes place, since maternal and paternal chromosome sets remain distinct until then? Or is it at the time of gastrulation when the embryonic chromosomes begin to take over from the maternal cytoplasm? Or a week after fertilisation when the embryo implants into the womb? Or what?

To join this argument is to involve oneself in circular reasoning if we accept the position put forward in this chapter about the nature of God's image in man. The Bible teaches that God chooses and cares for people; it is not concerned with embryological niceties. An excellent example of this is the Lord's word to Jeremiah (1.5): 'Before I formed you in the womb I knew you' (RSV) (cf. Eccles. 11.5; Isa. 44.2). This tells us about God's relationship to a person; it is as irrelevant to a scientific understanding of human physiology as is our Lord's admonition to Nicodemus about re-birth (John 3.3–6).

The only direct reference in Scripture to the value of foetal life is in Exodus 21.22 – 'When men strive together, and hurt a woman with child, so that there is a miscarriage, and yet no harm follows, the one who hurt her shall be fined, according as the woman's husband shall lay upon him' (RSV). The ways in which this verse has been interpreted show the importance (and danger) of preconceptions in interpreting Scripture. On the one hand it has been argued that abortion (albeit accidental miscarriage) was lightly regarded by the Mosaic law, and on the other that 'the life of a man's offspring is given a special value, and violence to it carries a penalty'.[30] The most influential statements of Christian attitudes to abortion are the Church of England's Board of Social Responsibility's *Abortion,*[31] R. F. R. Gardner's *Abortion: The Personal Dilemma*[32] and Oliver O'Donovan's *The Christian and the Unborn Child.*[33] Although they differ from one another in their views and conclusions, yet all three take their stand on the assumption that life is sacred. Oliver O'Donovan develops his ideas on the concept of 'individuation'. Other writers (particularly in the USA), have used the same basis for the notion of 'personhood' (which may be acquired only after, say, eight weeks of gestation have passed).

The idea of sacred life is acceptable if it means 'evocative of awe and commanding the utmost respect for the miracle that life is'. But if the word is used to mean absolute protection and inviolability, it becomes highly questionable. The traditional Western ethical tradition has been to give a foetus increasing protection as it develops;[34]

to go beyond this because of a greater knowledge of embryological processes is to introduce a new and debatable rigour. The argument of this chapter suggests that this rigour is not the only – or necessarily the most correct – interpretation of our biological knowledge.

The main point to emphasise is that good ethics are not likely to come from bad biology or naive theology. The fact is that we are biological machines, but also God's children. It is obviously wrong to deny this, but we are not helped in this area by confusing different methods of thought. The care of human life is, surely, a responsibility entrusted to us by God, and our attitude to the decisions that face us is an outworking of Christ's expectation for Christians encapsulated in the teaching about salt and light in the Sermon on the Mount.

Conclusion: genes and personality

Although it is true that we are the product of our genes, it is false to assert that we are nothing more than our genes. I have been concerned in this chapter to emphasise that we cannot claim that our behaviour or our personality is simply the result of the genes received from our parents. Of course they affect the person we are and influence the differences that distinguish us from other people. But someone who allows himself to be shaped entirely by his environments is like the unstable man who allows himself to be buffeted by the chances of fortune, and who will not 'receive anything from the Lord' (Jas. 1.6–8). An individual determined by his genes is not exercising the free will entrusted to him by his Creator.

How then do we reconcile our human diversity with the calling of Christ to be 'like him'? The answer must lie along two paths:

1. We must choose environments and seek God's grace in such a way that we allow him to mould us according to his purpose.

2. We have to recognise that God wants us to develop our own particular gifts for the good of his Church. I was brought up in an atmosphere that identified four levels of commitment. In descending order, these were commitments to overseas missionary work, to 'full-time Christian ministry', to teaching, and then the also-rans. This is pernicious: 'having gifts that differ according to the grace given to us, let us use them' (Rom. 12.6) (RSV).

This chapter has said little about specific personality traits; I will explore a series of examples in Chapter 5. I have been concerned here to show that genes do not *determine* our behaviour, and that we cannot be reduced to nothing more than an amalgam of gene products. Determinism and reductionism are among the more prevalent half-truths of our age; it is up to us to recognise them for what they are, and to search out the other half of the truth. Only then will we become mature . . . and like Christ.

Notes

1. See, for example, the three books produced for the National Evangelical Anglican Congress in Nottingham under the general title *Obeying Christ in a Changing World* (Collins, London, 1977).
2. Edward Wilson, *Sociobiology: The New Synthesis* (Harvard University Press, 1975).
3. John Hick, *Biology and the Soul* (Cambridge University Press, 1972).
4. See particularly *Science, Chance and Providence* (Oxford University Press, 1977) and his 1977 London Lectures already quoted by Malcolm Jeeves, *Human Science and Human Dignity* (Hodder & Stoughton, London, 1979).
5. Published in *Plain Christianity* (Epworth, London, 1954).
6. John Robinson, *Honest to God* (SCM, London, 1963).
7. See also A. R. Peacocke, *Creation and the World of Science* (Clarendon Press, Oxford, 1979).
8. Michael Polanyi, *Knowing and Being* (Routledge & Kegan Paul, London, 1969).
9. K. Barth, *Church Dogmatics* (T & T Clark, Edinburgh, 1961) Vol III pp. 327–9.
10. E. Brunner, *Man in Revolt* (Lutterworth, Guildford, 1939). p. 96.
11. C. F. D. Moule, *Man and Nature in the New Testament* (Athlone, London, 1964) p. 5.
12. H. D. MacDonald, *The Christian View of Man* (Marshall, Morgan & Scott, Basingstoke, 1981).
13. Cf. Francis Crick, *Life Itself: Its Origin and Nature* (Macdonald, 1982).
14. Cf. R. Griffiths, *The Human Use of Animals* (Grove Ethics Booklet, no. 46, 1982).
15. This second view is wholly independent of whether or not evolution has occurred. Many nineteenth-century scientists were convinced anti-evolutionists, but fully persuaded that the earth (and life) is millions of years old. Charles Lyell was a well-known supporter of this view.

16. It is extremely difficult to identify absolute differences between men and even the higher apes. Animals can learn, play, use tools, communicate, have nervous breakdowns, and are capable of a certain degree of abstract thought. One of the foremost animal behaviourists in Britain, W. H. Thorpe, has given particular attention to man–animal differences. He regards the only property of humans not found in animals as 'the recognition of abstract moral law' (*Biology, Psychology, and Belief*, Cambridge University Press, 1961).
17. It is possible to argue endlessly about hydatidiform moles, which are unique growths in the womb, but the majority (at least) are entirely male derived (from two sperm). They have no structure, and to all intents and purposes are degenerate pregnancies with a risk of becoming cancerous.
18. Jacques Monod, *Chance and Necessity* (Collins, London, 1972).
19. Robin Holliday, *The Science of Human Progress* (Oxford University Press, 1981).
20. Joseph Fletcher, *The Ethics of Genetic Control* (Doubleday, 1974).
21. W. Temple, *Readings in St. John's Gospel* (Macmillan, St. Martin's Library ed. 1968), p. 62.
22. In *Dictionary of Medical Ethics*, 2nd edn, edited by A. S. Duncan, G. R. Dunstan and R. B. Welbourn (Darton, Longman & Todd, London, 1981).
23. R. Snowden and G. D. Mitchell, *The Artificial Family* (Allen & Unwin, London, 1981) p. 121.
24. *Acta Obstet. Gynaecol. Scand.* vol. 61 (1982), p. 125.
25. *Med. J. Aust.*, vol. 1 (1982), p. 338.
26. Published in 1982.
27. In *Developments in Human Reproduction and Their Eugenic Ethical Implications* (Carter, C. O. (ed.) London, Academic, 1983).
28. See, for example, *Ethics of Fetal Research* (Yale University Press, 1975).
29. David Rorvik, *In His Image* (Hamish Hamilton, London 1978).
30. Harley Smyth, *Biblical Allusions to Life Before Birth* (Christian Medical Fellowship, 1975). The N.I.V. translation of Exodus 21:22 is as follows: 'If men who are fighting hit a pregnant woman and she gives birth prematurely but there is no serious injury, the offender must be fined. . . .'
31. Church Information Office, 1965.
32. Paternoster Press, Exeter, 1972.
33. Grove Ethics Booklet (1973), no. 1.
34. G. R. Dunstan, The moral status of the embryo: a tradition recalled *J. med. Ethics*, vol. 10 (1984) 38–44.

3: The grace of God

David Atkinson

The musical show *At the Drop of Another Hat* includes the delightful quotation by Michael Flanders of the old lady who said that 'If God had intended us to fly, he would never have given us the railways'. I want to put that beside this paragraph from Professor Steven Rose.

> Our genotype (that is, our genetic make-up) doesn't enable us to grow wings (and anyhow there are structural reasons why creatures with our body mass couldn't fly) and for a considerable portion of human history it has gone against nature for humans to fly. But today humans do fly – it is in some sense in our genotype to be able to modify our environment to transcend this limitation.[1]

Our very biology, this suggests, points beyond biology to other aspects of our human make-up: our creativity, our capacity for science, our technological skills. All this contributes to the fact that, despite Michael Flanders's old lady, we can buy an Airpass and transcend our biological limits.

But whether or not God 'intended us to fly', we are addressing ourselves in this chapter to the broader question: What has God got to do with what we do? In particular, what is the relation between God's grace and our personal freedom of action?

We are examining in this book both our human experience of freedom, and the variety of conditioning factors that limit our freedom, that affect how we behave, and that contribute to the differences between us. We have concentrated so far on the genetic basis of our personhood and on the conditioning effects of the social environment in which we grow. My task now is to place these influences of nature and nurture within the wider theological context of the grace of God. For Christians who believe in God, the fundamental conditioning factor of our behaviour – I shall suggest – is that it is *in Him* that 'we live and move and have our being.' My concern, therefore, will be primarily theological, but I shall be exploring throughout how the Christian faith links with the subject-matter of the first two chapters.

My theme in this chapter, then, is God's grace and personal freedom. My method will be first to look at our human experience of being persons, and at what we mean by personal freedom. Alongside this we will from a wider perspective stand on the ground of God's revelation in Christ and in Scripture, and sketch a theological framework of interpretation from which to try to understand our experiences of personal freedom. Then we shall explore the meaning of 'grace'. We will be taking many of our cues from the theology of St Paul, for, although I believe the Gospels share the same theology, Paul – especially in the letter to the Romans – is more systematic in his presentation. The basic presupposition of Paul's theology is the God of grace whom he experienced on the Damascus road. While his temperament and his background may well have been predisposing factors in the kind of religious experience he had, Paul himself believed that what happened was more than physical or emotional. He met the risen Jesus who spoke to him in Hebrew, giving him a vision of God's purpose for his ministry, and confronting him with a choice whether or not to be obedient to the heavenly vision (Acts 22.12–19). This encounter effected change in Paul. His values were different; his goals were different; his attitudes and behaviour were affected. And Paul attributed this dramatic – if untypical – experience to the grace of God. 'By the grace of God I am what I am' he wrote later (1 Cor.15.10) (RSV). Grace became a central word for Paul, and through his writings for the whole Christian tradition.

We must be alert to one particular danger as we proceed: that of slipping into a dualistic way of thinking that sees our relation to God as but one aspect of life, as though there were a 'scientific' part of life that interests geneticists and psychologists, and a 'religious' one that interests theologians. I do not believe that grace (like a certain widely advertised beer) merely 'refreshes the parts' that other disciplines cannot reach! Our theology of grace will try to point towards the way in which, so Christians believe, all of life at all levels is understood and lived from a centre in God.

What is 'person'?

In discussing personal freedom, we must begin with a closer look at what is meant by 'person'. My proposition here is that personhood includes an essentially religious dimension. Professor Stephen Evans writes:

> The rise of the human sciences in the twentieth century has been marked by the demise of the person. There is a definite tendency to avoid explanations of human behaviour which appeal to the conscious decisions of persons in favour of almost any non-personal factors.[2]

As both Professor Jeeves and Professor Berry have indicated, however, there are those within the sciences who acknowledge that there is something *irreducible* about human personhood; indeed that there is a series of levels at which the human person may and must be understood, each of them requiring its appropriate science and its appropriate methodology, but none of them explicable completely in terms of a 'lower' level. Each level – as the opening quotation from Steven Rose suggested – points beyond itself to 'higher' levels.[3]

In the simplest terms, we are at one level flesh and blood: physical, chemical *genetic* beings, 'of the dust of the earth'. This limits us so that, in terms of our physical make-up, we cannot fly. It also enables us: we could not act at all without a physical body. At a higher level, the 'dust of the earth' becomes a 'living being': this is the level of *biology*. At another level, we can think of our *relationship with our physical environment*. Man is placed 'in a garden': we are enriched or damaged by the environment in which we grow. At a higher level, we realise that being a person means being in *relation to other persons*, and this opens up new possibilities of love and hate, of reparation and forgiveness. It is not good that man should be alone. 'Guilt', 'shame', 'hope' and 'joy' are words that only have meaning within the context of personal relationship. Another level concentrates on *shared goals* and the mutual enrichment of a shared lifestyle. There is a whole area of attitudes and values, customs and morals. Then there is the level of *individual moral decision*. These higher levels closely interact: individual responsibility and corporate solidarity belong together. As the Old Testament in particular makes clear in its own terms, a person's behaviour may be shaped to a great extent through a person's relationship with others; he or she also has the responsibility of deciding for himself or herself how far to agree with, collude with, or react against, the patterns of others' expectancies.[4] Our personal values, attitudes and goals inform our decisions and are significant in our behaviour.

To return to Michael Flanders and the old lady: we would never have learned to fly, to transcend the possibilities laid down by the past, were it not for the vision, hope, patience, perseverance, problem-solving and long-range goals of the early pioneers. The point is well made by Anthony Storr.

> It is clear that it is as legitimate to ask towards what end a process is directed, as to inquire from what cause it originated, and I believe that any psychological description of human beings must attempt to answer both questions. The highly complicated facts of human behaviour can be related to both inquiries; and whilst some facts are better explained in terms of what has happened in the individual's past, others are more easily comprehended in terms of the goal towards which the individual appears to be striving. Neither description is complete without the other.[5]

Personhood, in other words, is – so to speak – 'directional'. The point of my earlier analysis is not to dissect us up into unrelated conceptual levels: precisely the opposite. It is to stress that each level points to an aspect of our human personhood that cannot adequately be understood without the total view.

The biblical meaning of the 'heart'

The theological basis for such a *holistic* view of personhood may be most easily grasped by noting the way in which both Old and New Testaments speak of 'the heart'. This theological term does not, as in common parlance, mean simply 'emotions'. In Scripture the 'heart' is a comprehensive term for the human personality as a whole, its inner life, its character. It is the conscious and deliberate spiritual activity of the whole human person. 'Heart' is the centre of man's feeling, understanding and willing. It is the source of bodily actions. It embraces the whole range of physical, emotional, intellectual and willing aspects of human personhood.[6] It points, in other words, to the essential *psychophysical unity* of the person, not in the sense that there is never disorder within the person (the contrary is true, as we shall see), but that each level of the person affects and is affected by all the others.

The 'heart-person' needs a body: there is an essential genetic base, both limiting action and enabling us to act. In order to act, the 'heart-person' needs an environment: there is an essential environmental determinant, both limiting action and enabling us to act. The 'heart' in biblical thinking is the mainspring of our behaviour.

Furthermore, the 'heart' in biblical usage is *directional*. It derives most of its meaning from that towards which it is directed. It is a *relational* word: our knowing, feeling, willing and acting are given meaning in relation to their objects. In other words, living is a process of interaction between the subjective 'heart' of the person, and the physical, social and spiritual environment in which his life history is made. In biblical thinking, therefore, personhood is *essentially religious*. That on which the 'heart' is centred, that from which we derive our values, that on which we place supreme worth – the object, that is, of our worship – is that which to some degree draws out from us our being, thinking, feeling and willing.

Christian theology speaks about the transcendent reality of the personal God from whom all human personhood derives its life and meaning. It underlines the essentially religious nature of personhood by saying that the 'heart' is always directed towards an object of worship, be that the living God or some sort of idol. St Paul, to whose theology of grace we shall shortly return, wrote of those who 'worshipped and served the creature rather than the Creator' (Rom. 1.25) (RSV).

In verse 20 Paul also noted that God's 'eternal power and deity' are seen in 'the things that have been made'. And that, we may judge, includes ourselves and the knowledge about human life and behaviour that we derive from the human sciences. Our human experience contains, if such knowledge is not suppressed,[7] what Peter Berger has aptly called 'signals of transcendence'.[8]

Just as watching snooker on a black-and-white telvision set ('Pot Grey') illustrates how what we do experience points beyond itself to another dimension of the game which (unless we change our receiver) we are as yet unable fully to apprehend, so many human experiences point beyond themselves to something more.

By 'signals of transcendence' in this sense, I do not mean only the evidence of widespread religious experience as documented for example by Sir Alistair Hardy[9] or by David Hay.[10] Nor do I mean only the spiritual hunger that grows within some secular systems.[11] I mean also the fact that science works at all points to a correspondence between the mind of man and a principle of rationality and order in the universe,[12] and that the sense of moral outrage we feel at the shooting of a headmaster in front of his class 'cries out to heaven'[13] – there is an objective sense of 'wrong' to which we appeal. I mean that what Abraham Maslow calls 'peak experiences'[14] of ecstatic joy, and we might add moments of deepest grief, give us a perception of reality that transcends time. Another example is that our fear of death can give rise to a death-refusing hope that life is more than this.[15] These common experiences of living point beyond themselves to a transcendent reality. They act, I would suggest, as confirmers of the view that human personhood, the 'heart', has an essentially religious dimension.

What is 'freedom'?

I move now from the question of 'person' to the question of 'freedom'. My proposition here is that from a Christian theological perspective, personal freedom means freedom of a 'heart' that is directed towards God.

Within the different constraints on us at the different levels of our personhood, there are obviously different sorts of freedom. At the physical level, we can experience the same sort of freedom as inanimate objects: if stones or people drop from aeroplanes, they can 'fall freely'. At the social level, there is the sort of freedom of those who might say 'We are not bound by the customs of others, we are free to decide for ourselves'. Both Professor Jeeves and Professor Berry have argued that within the constraints of our genetic and cultural inheritance, there is a true freedom of choice. But to give full meaning to 'freedom', we need another focus for the ellipse. While there is a freedom *from,* there is also a freedom *for*. As John Macmurray argues,[16], a thing is truly free if it acts spontaneously from within in accordance with what is real. The man who in the pain of a marital trauma seeks the freedom of divorce *from* a bad marriage, may yet find himself bound by feelings of guilt, bereavement, depression and loneliness, and not be free 'within' *for* a more satisfying life.

This freedom 'within' I would like to call 'freedom of the heart'. The paradox of life is that we experience *both* that we have a measure of freedom of choice and of responsibility within limits, of striving towards goals, *and* that all this is limited. It is limited by its origin and by its context, as the previous chapters have illustrated. It is also, I suggest, limited 'within', in the 'heart', in a personal incapacity to live freely.

Here are some instances of what I mean.

One of the things that hinders personal freedom is a sense of inner *disorientation and disorder*. Much contemporary psychotherapy is working with a sense of personal disorder. The intellect pulls one way; the feelings another. Within the psychophysical unity of the person in which all levels affect the other, there is a sense of discord and not harmony. We sometimes want to do what is right, but 'evil lies close at hand' (cf. Rom. 7.21) (RSV). After describing the story of his turbulent adolescence, Augustine says 'Such was my life: was it life?'

In his analysis of the human condition in his epistle to the Romans, St Paul uses the picture of several paralysing 'powers' to illustrate his theme that without the grace of God man is essentially disordered. He writes of *sin* – that disorder of relationship between man and God that is expressed in the disruption of man's relationships with others, with his environment and within himself. Here we need to think not primarily of personal acts of wrong, but of the radical misdirection of the 'heart'. In biblical theology, we have said, man's real freedom is experienced when the 'heart' is centred on God. Paradoxically, Christian freedom is found in service. When the 'heart' is directed away from God, we are 'in the service of sin'. When the 'heart' is directed to the service of God, then man is 'free'. The 'power of sin' is often expressed under three headings: 'the world, the flesh and the devil'. When the New Testament speaks of 'flesh' it often means human nature considered in opposition to God. When it speaks of 'the world' it often means the course of human events determined by men through whose fallenness sin is perpetuated. In other words, we need to give full place to the ways in which other peoples' disorders can affect a person, and to the emotional and spiritual wounds that come from experiencing wrong from others.[17] We must think also of the way wrong can be institutionalised in unjust structures within the social environment and on the global scene. 'The devil' points us to the fact that we live within a spiritual universe in which evil can affect us. The 'world, the flesh and the devil' are part of our environment, and can be determinants of our behaviour.

A second of the paralysing factors that hinders personal freedom is *guilt*. Whether we read Freud, Rollo May, Hobart Mowrer or their disciples, most schools of psychology recognise the inhibiting effects of guilt, whether understood as pathological, illusory or real. We need to distinguish psychologial 'guilt feelings' from what Martin Buber calls 'existential guilt',[18] which occurs when someone 'injures an order of the human world whose foundation he knows and recognises as those of his own existence and of all common existence'. We are confronted, in other words, with the sense of a moral order before which we perceive ourselves to stand under threat. This corresponds with the second of the powers to which St Paul refers: the 'law'. By this he means the holy character of God to which the moral prescriptions of the Pentateuch and the inner accusations of conscience point. We can develop this to speak of the sense of condemnation we can feel when confronted with what we know to be the moral imperative of God's presence.

A third aspect of our humanity – and the third of Paul's 'powers' – that holds us in its grip and hinders our freedom is 'death', especially the fear of death and of non-being: the fear captured by those haunting words 'We die only once and for such a long time'. The fear of death may put limits to the freedom of life. As Helmut Thielicke put it: It is the man who has confidence and hope for his last hour who has no need to fear the next minute.

Are not disorder, guilt and fear universal human experiences? And do they not put constraints on personal freedom? If we are going to speak of personal freedom of behaviour in the context of the essentially religious nature of personhood, we need to take issue with those powers of 'sin', 'law' and 'death' to which Paul refers. A theological understanding of freedom concentrates not so much on the freedom from external constraints, as on the freedom 'of the heart'; a freedom *for* life lived freely before what is ultimately real – that is, God.

What is 'grace'?

It is in the context of his discussion of 'sin', 'law' and 'death' that St Paul writes about 'grace'. What is grace?

We must acknowledge immediately that 'grace' is an umbrella word under which many different emphases shelter.[19] Some theologians (for example, some of the Apostolic Fathers) understood grace rather like a medicine from God dispensed through the sacramental life of the Church. Others (especially Augustine and some strands of Protestant thinking) understood grace in a more surgical way: God cutting out the inner root of sin. Many in the Catholic tradition have understood grace as a sort of second tier added on to our nature.

In all these models there is a tendency to a rather mechanical view of grace. By contrast, for Paul grace is fundamentally a *relational* word. God calls us to share a gracious relationship with himself.[20] It is in what we might call the 'heart to heart' conversation, which God initiates by grace, that he creates freedom from some of the effects of the paralysing powers, and creates freedom for learning to live the free life with our 'hearts' centred in worship on him.

I want to analyse this relational understanding of grace under three headings.

The grace of creation and providence

The belief in 'God the Creator and Preserver of all mankind' lies behind all biblical views of the world. God is not thought of as part of the world process, but stands over it in sovereign freedom. God speaks his word, and from nothing something is made. Further, the order of creation is not a logically necessary order that we could discover by thinking from an armchair. It is rather a *contingent* order – that is, God could have made it different. The universe is derived from God and is held in being by him.[21]

What does all this imply?

First, that there is a rational unity to the universe. It is this that makes science possible, and gives the undergirding to the possibility of, for example, psychology and genetics.

Secondly, the contingence of the universe makes science necessary. Discoveries are not made by *a priori* logical connections, but by experimenting and observing.

Thirdly, we cannot operate only at the level of physical determinism. This is the theological basis for the rejection of reductionism. Each level of personal life as it comes to view through scientific inquiry needs relations with other levels to give it coherence and meaning. At this point the wonder of the Christian understanding of the Incarnation takes on a fresh light. T. F. Torrance understands one significance of the expression 'becoming flesh' as a 'vertical dimension' which gives 'the horizontal co-ordinates of the universe the integrative factor, providing them with consistent and ultimate meaning.'[22] In our psychology and our genetics, as indeed in all sciences, we are in touch at a certain level with part of the meaning of 'the Word made flesh'.

Fourthly, the fact of creation implies that life is a gift.[23] The gift of personal freedom is thus linked to our creaturely dependence on the Creator and to living, as Macmurray said, spontaneously before what is Real, namely God.

Finally, the freedom of the creation is a contingent freedom, ultimately grounded in the sovereign freedom of God. Our personal freedom, in other words, is not irrational arbitrariness. It is rather a limited freedom within the spatial, temporal and personal boundaries of a universe derived from and dependent on God. The fundamental conditioning factor on our behaviour is that it is in him that we live and move and have our being.

By 'providence' Christians mean that God has not wound his world up and now stands idly by to see if it will go. Rather, in gracious care, he is actively sustaining his world in being. God has not abandoned the world to the disordering effects of evil. Rather, he is upholding it by 'the word of his power' (Heb. 1.3), restraining within it the destructive effects of wrong. Abraham Kuyper, following Calvin, spoke of this as God's 'common grace': 'the omnipresent operation of divine mercy which reveals itself everywhere where human hearts are found to beat'.[24] God in grace restrains evil, and provides a context in which life can develop more fully and richly. We are therefore, we may judge, to discern the hand of a gracious God behind the many and varied ways in which evil is held back and the good of mankind promoted: in the work of the artist and the scientist; in the skill of the doctor; in the healing relationship provided by the therapist; in the seeking for justice in social structures and a more equitable distribution of earth's resources by citizens and politicians. Despite the deterministic pressures of a broken world, the Christian faith affirms that God is creating a context in which personal freedom of the 'heart' can become more possible.

Covenant grace

God not only turns towards his world in grace (which incidentally gives us a strong incentive to turn towards it in scientific exploration), but in particular he turns towards his people. In the Old Testament covenants, God takes an initiative of love towards his people and promises himself to them as their God.

Two Old Testament words in particular convey what the New Testament means by 'grace'. The word *chen* refers to the favour that God bestows in sovereign freedom. For example, 'Noah found *favour* in the eyes of the Lord' (Gen. 6.8) (RSV). The other word, *hesed,* is the central word of covenant 'loving kindness'. It is used of God's loyal and faithful commitment to his people, that he would be their God and that they would be his people. *Hesed* love becomes the foundation of the people's life and relationships. *Hesed* is expressed through the gracious act of God in choosing Israel to be his own. Even though, as the story of Hosea illustrates, Israel proves unfaithful, God remains true and trustworthy. As H. R. Mackintosh put it: 'Grace is love in its princely and sovereign form, love to the indifferent and the disloyal, whose one claim is their need.'[25]

Furthermore, as the story of Hosea also makes clear, the God who comes in *hesed* is the God who is 'righteous'. Righteousness and love, grace and justice belong together. And the covenant people who in grace are called into the freedom of being God's people, are required to express their freedom in obedience to him, and to reflect in their actions something of his character. They are free to be different from what they were; they are commanded to be different in their behaviour, in response to grace. For example in the Holiness Code of Leviticus 19, all the levels of life touched on – domestic, religious, economic, agricultural, personal – link the duties of the people to the constant refrain 'I am the Lord'. Freedom, as we said before, is understood in terms of loving service to the covenant Lord.

To return to our discussion of 'common grace', one of the areas of life in which the people of God were to display in their behaviour something of the meaning of covenant grace, was the care for the poor, and the quest for social justice. To affirm the covenant grace of God should commit us also to such active concern.

Finally, God's gracious relationship with his people is not dependent on any quality in them. God's grace, though requiring their response, is not conditioned by it. 'It was not because you were more in number than any other people that the Lord set his love upon you . . . it is because the Lord loves you' (Deut. 7.7) (RSV). Personal life is given its value, in other words, not because of any quality of life, or 'indicators of personhood' that are intrinsic to the person, but as a gift. Personal dignity is, in Barth's word, an 'alien dignity'. We need to keep that in mind in discussion of ethical themes in which definitions of personhood are central.

The grace of redemption

Here my theme is that the grace of God *became event* in Christ.

The centre of the Old Covenant is God's act of redemption at the Exodus. One of the primary biblical convictions about God is that he is a God who *acts*. It is this sense of the living and active God, from whom all other reality and activity originate, that must infuse our understanding of grace. As the consciousness of being God's covenant people developed, the future action of God in history became increasingly significant. The time would come, God promised through the later prophets, when 'a new heart I will give you' (Ezek. 36.26) and 'I will write my law – my character – upon your heart' (Jer. 31.33).

When we turn to the New Testament, that promise is understood in terms of the reality within our history of the action of God's love in the person and work of Christ. St Paul writes of 'God's love' being 'poured into our hearts by the Holy Spirit' (Rom. 5.5). The theme of the covenant comes to its most vivid expression – the Incarnation. Unmistakably now, God is *for us*.

There is therefore a continuity in the New Testament with the covenant theme of the Old. The acts of God at the Exodus and throughout covenant history can be understood as pointing forward to this decisive moment in which the divine grace was embodied in a person: the Word became flesh, and his glory was seen, full of grace and truth (John 1.14).

But there is something decisively new here also. What God in the Old Covenant *requires*, that in Christ he also *gives*. If the primary emphasis of the Old is about a right relation with God required in response to grace, the primary emphasis in the New is about a right relation with God offered as a gift of grace.

In Christ, says Paul, a new world is disclosed, which has established a new way of living within this world's history. It is centred on the cross and resurrection of Christ. The 'grace of God has appeared for the salvation of all men' (Titus 2.11) (RSV). In Christ – to return to our thinking about the freedom of the 'heart' – we see the *Free Man*.

In Paul's mind, grace is often set over against other factors that affect human behaviour. He sets grace over against the 'power of sin' (Rom. 5.20) and over against the law, understood as a condemning moral code (Rom. 6.14f.) Grace gives a new principle of life over against the rule of death (Rom. 5.21). Indeed through grace Paul speaks of 'freedom' from the three paralysing powers that we considered earlier. Romans 6 is about freedom from the power of sin; Romans 7 about freedom from the condemnation of law; Romans 8 about freedom from the fear of death. And at the end of each of these chapters he writes 'through Jesus Christ our Lord'.

Grace is understood as replacing a religion of moral striving through human resources (Rom. 11.6). Grace stands against all human systems of values (2 Cor. 1.12). For Paul the gospel was a 'gospel of the grace of God' (Acts 20.24). As the beginning and ending of all the letters that bear his name make clear, grace is 'from God our Father', 'through Jesus Christ our Lord'.

How, then, are we to understand the relation between God's grace and our personal freedom? By looking at the Free Man, Jesus Christ. In him we glimpse the reality of what human life is intended to be. In him, God's grace 'has appeared'.

Furthermore, the way in which the grace of God touches human nature is to be understood by the way God has acted in grace through Christ: that is *through death and resurrection*. The grace of

God that is personally embodied in Jesus only has meaning through the way of the cross and the empty tomb.

If Torrance is right in seeing the incarnation as the 'vertical dimension', giving meaning and coherence to all the levels of human personhood, then grace touches human nature at all these levels, and does so through death and resurrection.Grace, therefore, does not replace nature – as some Protestants have taught. Nor is grace added to nature, as some in the Catholic tradition believe. Grace 'perfects' nature without abolishing it, but this is only through death and resurrection. Taking the resurrection body of Jesus as our guide, this means continuity, enrichment and transformation.

How does grace affect our behaviour?

It is all very well to speak of the event of Christ: but how does that touch the individual Christian believer? We return to the picture that St Paul draws in his letter to the Romans, especially in chapter 5. Here the paralysing powers of sin, law and death discussed in chapters 1–4 are described as 'the age of Adam'. Into the continuity of human history breaks the event of Christ, inaugurating a renewed humanity within our world: 'the age of Christ'. Thereafter the two 'ages' run consecutively. The Christian believer is held in the tension of the two 'ages'. He is 'in Adam'; he is 'in Christ'. He is, in other words, in process of being transformed, through *death* to the old 'nature', and through *resurrection* into the new.

There is, therefore, both a continuity and a discontinuity between the Christian's life and other human life. Helmut Thielicke puts it this way:

> The relation is one of continuity in so far as they eat and drink, marry and are given in marriage, laugh and cry, stand under authorities and within orders (and, we might add, are to some extent determined by the genetic base of their personhood and the conditioning effects of their cultural environments); it is one of discontinuity because they *no longer receive their orientation from all this*.[26]

In other words, their 'heart' is directed elsewhere. This 'dual environment' of the Christian is captured well by the double description of the writer's location in the letter to the Ephesians – he is 'in chains' (Eph. 6.20) with reference to his physical situation; he is 'in the heavenly places in Christ Jesus' (Eph. 2.6) with reference to the direction of his 'heart'.

The Christian is a free person to the extent that he is united to Christ, the Free Man. He is still within a fallen world; he is still open to the wounds of others' sins and the temptations of his own; he still lives within the limits of time and space, and of physical and social determinants. He will still die. But united with Christ, his 'heart' is now directed towards the worship and service of God. He is learning to be free to be different. The practical question for the Christian is: how does the grace of Christ effect freedom?

Here are five preliminary points, after which I want to be more practical.

First, we are thinking of how God's grace is actually experienced in our daily lives, and that is often spoken of in the New Testament as the work of the Holy Spirit. 'God's love has been poured into our hearts through the Holy Spirit which has been given to us' (Rom. 5.5) (RSV).

Secondly, we are thinking of a richly varied constellation of experiences: what St Peter called God's 'dappled' or 'many coloured' grace (1 Pet. 4.10). The Holy Spirit does not create Christian clones. Rather he creates whole new vistas of rich personal variety. This is emphasised by the use of the body metaphor in the New Testament, describing the Church as a organism of diversity within unity. As 'grace is given to each', (Eph. 4.7), so there are varieties of gifts, varieties of service, varieties of working, though all 'inspired by one and the same Spirit' (1 Cor. 12.4–11).

Thirdly, all experiences of the Holy Spirit's gracious activity in the human 'heart' are *human* experiences. They occur in this world in people whose persons are the complexity of levels we have indicated. And we do not all travel the Damascus road. God calls us into a gracious relationship with himself, from all our different starting points, and at all the different levels of our personhood. If we are to discern God's grace, therefore, it will be in and through the agencies of temperament, attitude and personal history; and there will be a many-levelled physiological, psychological and personal base to our relationship with him. In other words, there is a genuine pluralism in the experience of God's grace. We should expect to find 'varieties' of behaviour.

Fourthly, the way the grace of Christ comes to us in the Spirit is most often within the fellowship of the Christian Church. The early Church was built on fellowship and mutual ministry, breaking bread, apostolic teaching and prayer. These are some of the 'means of grace' by which the Holy Spirit brings God's gracious action in Christ into touch with day-to-day experience. And the Holy Communion most clearly signifies the way in which the natural things of bread and wine can become vehicles for the present gracious activity of God. Here we are invited to 'lift up our hearts'; and we are assured of the 'forgiveness of our sins and all other benefits of his passion'.

Fifthly, a growing relationship is a process and takes time. While Paul says that where the Spirit of the Lord is there is freedom, he couples this with a reminder of the process of growth, of being changed 'from one degree of glory to another' (2 Cor. 3.18). And growth – especially by way of death and resurrection – is often the way of suffering and pain, not only of joy. The grace of the cross is not cheap; the way of grace will be costly for us. Let us conclude, then, by returning to some of the different levels of our personhood, and see what it means for grace to touch these levels through death and resurrection.

Attitude, goals and aims

I begin with the level of our *attitudes, goals and aims*. Paul's question 'Who will deliver me from this body of death?' – in which he felt so morally incapacitated, – he answered himself: 'Thanks be to God through Jesus Christ our Lord!' (Rom. 7.24,25) (RSV). Later he wrote of 'putting on the Lord Jesus Christ' (Rom. 13.14), to indicate that the Christian's moral incapacity is provided for in Christ. Christian behaving is not adherence to a moral code. Christian faith does not only point towards the good; it also offers this charismatic dimension of inner resource. Where other ethical systems look towards the vision of a new person and urge 'Be what you are not', Paul's understanding of grace reminds him that 'You *are* a new person in Christ, so be what you are!'

The exercise of this new moral resource is, though, a matter of habit, of learning, of growth. Believers are those who – so the writer to the Hebrews indicates – have their faculties 'trained by practice to distinguish good from evil' (Heb. 5.14). And that practice comes by Christian living within the Christian community and in the wider society.

This is part of what Paul means, I think, by 'refusing to allow the world to squeeze us into its own mould', but rather that we 'be transformed' by the renewal of our minds (Rom. 12.2). Here the resurrection theme comes to the fore again: 'Put off your old nature . . . be renewed in the spirit of your minds, and put on the new nature, created after the likeness of God' (Eph. 4.22f.) (RSV). If you *have been* raised with Christ, seek the things that are above (Col. 3.1). Whatever is true, honourable, just, pure, lovely, gracious . . . think about these things . . . and the God of peace will be with you. (Phil. 4.8f.).

And whereas this comes to us in the form of moral imperatives, which require the pain, the struggle and the death as well as the resurrection of growth, as we 'work out our salvation with fear and trembling', grace reminds us that 'God is at work in us, both to will and to work for his good pleasure' (Phil. 2.13) (RSV).

This is part of our freedom from 'the world'. And we all know those who from Zacchaeus onwards have found that an encounter with Christ has changed their priorities, their values and their attitudes.

Personal relationships

Secondly, let us think about resurrection *at the level of our personal relationships*. After speaking about the individual renewal of the mind, St Paul in Romans 12 goes on immediately to speak about the style of personal relationships within the Christian community (chapter 12), about responsibilities of citizenship within the world (chapter 13), and about recognising the varieties of different constraints on us in our respect for one another's consciences (chapter 14). Conscience will be our theme in Chapter 6, and our glance at common grace indicated the importance of social responsibility (to which we cannot give further space now). Our present concern is individual personal behaviour in relation with others.

Paul's emphasis here and elsewhere is that the gospel of grace should inform and mould our relations with others. In other words, in all our 'covenants' of life with life, we are to find ways of expressing something of God's gracious covenant with us. The fact of

God's gracious relationship with us is both a pattern and a resource for our relationships with one another.

Let me give you two instances of what I mean.

In the husband/wife covenant relationship of a marriage, about which Dr Jack Dominian has helpfully written,[27] an opportunity is provided in the close new relationship for the healing of emotional wounds from the past. Each partner comes to marriage with personal needs. Marriage, says Dr Dominian, can – through God's grace – become an environment of nourishment, healing and growth. Each can be to the other a minister of grace. The marriage covenant can – as it grows through all its pains and joys in time – be a visible expression of what God's covenant with his people is about.[28] It is, in other words, in the service – the bond – of marriage, as both learn to give themselves in love, each for the sake of the other, that personal and mutual freedom can grow.

Marriage is a paradigm of other, less intimate, relationships within the Christian community. But in each we are called on to display as appropriate (and the grace is given to us to make it possible) a quality of relationship that itself expresses costly self-giving for the sake of the other. Grace can, in such ways, *overcome handicaps of our nurture*. Christian counselling also can be a context in which the pains of early hard relationships can be eased, and some of the paralysing pressure of sin – others', as well, sometimes, as our own – can give way to liberty.

Related to this, the other example I would give is that of *forgiveness*. Here is a prayer, quoted by Dr Martin Israel, found on a piece of paper near the body of a dead child in Ravensbruck Nazi concentration camp:

> O Lord,
> Remember not only the men and women of goodwill but also those of illwill.
> But do not only remember the suffering they have inflicted on us; remember the fruits we bought, thanks to this suffering:
> our comradeship, our loyalty, our humility, the courage, the
> generosity, the greatness of heart which has grown out of all
> this. And when they come to judgement, let all the fruits
> we have borne be their forgiveness.[29]

Could that have been written, other than by grace? Forgiveness recognises wrong as wrong, but refuses to let that wrong for ever hold us in the bondage of resentment and bitterness. Forgiveness is one of the clearest marks of grace in personal relationships.

The physical and biological

Finally, at *the physical and biological level:* does grace reach there too? For all of us the 'resurrection of the body' is still to come; we still bear in our bodies the frailty of our fallenness; we will still die. Even in this life, God does sometimes touch the body with his grace, bringing physical healing. But even when, like Epaphroditus, Trophimus, Timothy, Paul himself, there remains through life some physical infirmity, grace can overcome *the handicaps of nature* by transforming our relationship to our body.

Whether we think of Paul himself, or much nearer home someone like Joni Eareckson,[30] there can be in the despair of apparently unanswered prayer for release from infirmity, the freedom brought to us by the words 'My grace is sufficient for you' (2 Cor. 12.9). Certainly also the change in our attitudes can have profound effects on our physical bodies, as psychosomatic medicine from Flanders Dunbar onwards has affirmed. The writer of Proverbs 3.7 said so centuries before: 'Fear the Lord, and turn away from evil. It will be healing to your flesh and refreshment to your bones'.

Again here, we need to emphasise our differences. God does not deal with each person in an identical manner. Sometimes he withholds healing at one level of life in order to heal in other ways first. Yet with all our variety, we have a common hope that the day will come when he will change this our lowly body to be like his resurrection body, by the power which enables him to subdue all things to himself (Phil. 3.21).

At all levels, then, grace can touch us, through costly death and the transformation of resurrection. Growth in freedom comes through putting to death the old nature, and by living the risen life. It is a process, with its pains and frustrations, within the tension of the two ages. The Puritan concentration on the New Testament metaphors of warfare and conflict reminds us of one pole of that tension. The charismatic emphasis on the New Creation in Christ points to the other. But the confidence and hope that is born of grace is that our struggle here is part of a process by which God is transforming the whole person – the 'heart' – drawing us continually into a gracious relationship with himself, in which gradually we can learn to set the worship of our 'hearts' more fully upon him. That is our Christian freedom; it is found in the service of God and, with his gracious help, in the service of our neighbour.

And our Christian confidence is that the sufferings of this present time are not worth comparing with the glory that is to be revealed. The whole creation waits with eager longing for the revealing of the sons of God. The creation was subjected to futility, but will one day be set free from its bondage to decay, and will obtain the glorious freedom of the children of God (Rom. 8.18f.).

Notes

1. *The Guardian,* 6th May, 1982. (my square brackets)
2. Stephen Evans, *Preserving the Person* (IVP, Leicester 1979), p. 14.
3. This is worked out persuasively by Michael Polanyi in 'Life's Irreducible Structure', in *Knowing and Being* (Routledge & Kegan Paul, London, 1969); cf. also David Martin, 'The Status of the Human Person in the Behavioural Sciences', in R. H. Preston (ed.), *Technology and Social Justice* (SCM, London, 1971).
4. Cf., for example, W. Eichrodt, *Theology of the Old Testament,* Vol. 2, Ch. XX: 'The Individual and the Community in the Old Testament God-Man Relationship' (ET. SCM, London, 1967).
5. Anthony Storr, *The Integrity of the Personality* (Pelican, Harmondsworth, 1963), p. 28. Cf. also G. W. Allport, *Becoming* (Yale, 1955), pp. 47ff.
6. Cf. H. W. Wolff, *Anthropology of the Old Testament* (SCM, London, 1974); 'Heart' in C. Brown (ed.), *Dictionary of New Testament Theology,* Vol. II (Paternoster Press, Exeter, 1976); R. Bultmann, *Theology of the New Testament,* Vol. I (SCM, London, 1952 E.T.), p. 220f.
7. A point discussed at the end of David Hay's fascinating study of religious experience: *Exploring Inner Space* (Pelican, Harmondsworth, 1981).
8. Peter Berger, *A Rumour of Angels* (Allen Lane, Harmondsworth, 1969), p. 70.
9. Alistair Hardy, *The Spiritual Nature of Man* (Clarendon Press, Oxford, 1979).
10. David Hay, *Exploring Inner Space* (Pelican, Harmondsworth, 1981).
11. Such as that documented in Trevor Beeson's study of Euro-Marxism, *Discretion and Valour* (Collins (Fount), London, 1974; revised 1982).

12. Cf. A. R. Peacocke, *Science and the Christian Experiment* (Oxford University Press, 1971), pp. 133f.
13. Cf. Berger, *A Rumour of Angels,* op. cit., p. 85.
14. Cf. Abraham Maslow, *The Farther Reaches of Human Nature* (Pelican, Harmondsworth, 1971).
15. Cf. the growth in certainty of belief in an afterlife with increasing old age: M. Argyle and B. Beit-Hallahmi, *The Social Psychology of Religion* (Routledge & Kegan Paul, London, 1975), p. 69.
16. John Macmurray, *Freedom in the Modern World* (Faber, London, 1932, 1968).
17. The 'sins of the fathers' can be 'visited on the children' (cf. Exod. 20.5).
18. Martin Buber, 'Guilt and Guilt Feelings', *Psychiatry,* vol. 20, no. 1 (February 1957) p. 117.
19. T. F. Torrance, *The Doctrine of Grace in the Apostolic Fathers* (Oliver & Boyd, Edinburgh, 1948); R. Haight, *The Experience and Language of Grace* (Gill & Macmillan, Dublin, 1979); W. Oates (ed.), *Basic Writings of Saint Augustine,* Vol. I (Random House, New York, 1948); A. M. Fairweather (ed.), *Aquinas on Nature and Grace* (Library of Christian Classics, Westminster Press, Philadelphia, 1954); Karl Rahner, *Nature and Grace* (Sheed & Ward, London, 1963); E. J. Yarnold, *The Second Gift* (St Paul Publications, Slough, 1974); C. Ryder Smith, *The Bible Doctrine of Grace* (Epworth, London, 1956).
20. Cf. John Oman, *Grace and Personality* (Cambridge University Press, 1917; Fontana edn 1960).
21. Cf. T. F. Torrance, *Divine and Contingent Order* (Oxford University Press, 1981).
22. Ibid., p. 24.
23. Or, as Barth puts it, a 'loan'. *Church Dogmatics* (T & T Clark, English trans. 1961), Vol. III, No. 4, p. 324.
24. Quoted in C. van Til, *Common Grace* (Presbyterian and Reformed Publishing Company, 1947), pp. 14ff.
25. Quoted in Torrance, *The Doctrine of Grace in the Apostolic Fathers* op. cit.
26. Helmut Thielicke, *Theological Ethics* (A & C Black, London, 1968), Vol. 1: 'Foundations', p. 40. (my square brackets)
27. Cf. Jack Dominian, *Marriage Faith and Love* (Darton, Longman & Todd, London, 1981).
28. Cf. David Atkinson, *To Have and To Hold* (Collins, London, 1979).
29. Martin Israel, *The Pain that Heals* (Hodder & Stoughton, London, 1981), p. 114.
30. The story of Joni's Christian faith – a faith that held her through the

trials of coming to terms with paralysis following a swimming accident – is told in the book which bears her name, *Joni,* by Joni Eareckson (Pickering & Inglis, Glasgow, 1976).

PART II THREE CASE STUDIES

4: Religion

Malcolm Jeeves

We noted in Chapter 1 how psychologists, along with most biologists, adopt some form of what I called 'methodological determinism' in going about their daily work and in constructing their theories. We also noted that among psychologists a wide variety of views are evident when it comes to building models to explain and predict aspects of behaviour. Some confine their models to talking about the physiological, biochemical and neurological bases of behaviour. Others talk in terms of information flow models. Yet others are more concerned with social aspects of behaviour and the influences of one individual upon another and of the group upon the individual. I argued that, as far as I can see, there is nothing from within psychological science that can deny the reality of freedom of choice. I also explained how most psychologists accept the need to study behaviour at a number of different and distinguishable 'levels'. This point was elaborated by David Atkinson in the last chapter. We now begin a series of case studies. In this chapter, we focus our attention on religion, and especially on differences in religious belief, experience and behaviour. What can be said in general terms about the study of behaviour and belief can be applied in particular to studies of religious behaviour and beliefs. Once again, we can ask how did it come that we find such variety in religious behaviour and religious belief? We can ask questions about the determinants of religious belief and of unbelief. We can ask what function religious beliefs serve for the individual and for the group. As we ask these questions, we shall again face the fact of relativism in beliefs that we touched upon in Chapter 1.

There are two remaining issues that it would be sensible to deal with at once so that they do not distract from what follows.

First, as we examine the variety of determinants of religious belief, experience and behaviour, is it the case that we explain them away as we identify their probable psychological roots and origins? The answer is an unambiguous 'no'. Just as we do not judge the truth or falsity of the beliefs held by an historian, a mathematician or a scientist by an analysis of their psychological origins, but by critically weighing the appropriate evidence in each case, so with religious beliefs we judge their truth by examining the relevant evidence. In a word, origins tell us nothing about truth value when it comes to assessing beliefs or, for that matter, unbeliefs. For unbelief has psychological roots just as assuredly as belief.

Secondly, you will notice that we move rapidly from explanations at one psychological level to those at another. The classic example of this is the psychological study of conversion. You may study it at the psycho-physiological level, as Dr William Sargant did in *Battle for the Mind*[1] and *The Mind Possessed*.[2] You may study it at the psycho-dynamic level, as Freud did in *The Future of an Illusion*.[3] Or you may study it at the social psychological level by looking at the effects of group pressures and pressures to conformity. All this I have done elsewhere.[4] Religious experiences and behaviour are of such complexity that we need all these levels to begin to understand them. These levels should be viewed as complementary, and not as competitors either to one another or to the accounts given in personal and religious terms that were discussed in the last chapter by Dr Atkinson.

Religious belief, experience and behaviour

Just as in Chapter 1 I pointed out that to do full justice to the topic I would need to range over the whole of contemporary psychology, so now to do justice to this chapter's topic I would need to give an account of the whole of the psychology of religion. Clearly, this is impossible. However, just as in the first chapter I drew upon examples from psychology to illustrate the points I was making about determinants of behaviour in general, whether from the 'bottom-up' or the 'top-down' approach, so this time I shall draw upon the literature on the psychology of religion to illustrate the way in which psychologists understand the main determinants of religious beliefs, behaviour and experience.

In what follows we shall consider four main areas. First, differences in religious belief and behaviour that may be related to personality factors and to child-rearing practices. Secondly, different kinds of belief and behaviour that we see in people at successive stages of the life cycle from infancy to old age. Thirdly, differences in belief and behaviour that seem to be closely associated with particular denominational attachments. And fourthly, differences that do little more than reflect prevailing and passing fashions or emphases.

After reviewing these various determinants, we shall return to a central question: how as Christians do we decide what constitutes authentic Christian belief and authentic Christian behaviour? Lest you think this is a very simple question, let me illustrate it from an historical point of view, following the line taken by Professor Andrew Walls of Aberdeen University when he gave a lecture in 1981 entitled, 'The Gospel as the Prisoner and Liberator of Culture'.[5]

Professor Walls invited us to imagine a long-living scholarly space visitor who was given a research grant to make periodic visits to the planet Earth to study the behaviour of Christians living there. When he came to Earth in AD 37, he visited Jerusalem and noted that almost without exception the Jerusalem Christians were Jews, met in a temple, offered animal sacrifices, kept the seventh day free from work, circumcised their male children, and delighted in reading certain old law books. In fact, they appeared to be one of several denominations of Judaism. What distinguished them from the other sects was that they identified an important figure, namely Jesus of Nazareth, who had recently been crucified, as the same person referred to in their law books as the Messiah, the Son of Man, and the Suffering Servant.

Returning in AD 325, our space traveller came to Nicea, and there he saw a great meeting of Church leaders. There was scarcely a Jew among them. Indeed, they seemed rather hostile to Jews, were horrified at the thought of animal sacrifices, treated the seventh day as an ordinary working day and instead had various special religious observances on the first day. While they used the law books of the Jerusalem Christians, they also had another set of writings to which they gave equal weight and authority. They were also now using titles like 'Son of God' and 'Lord' to talk about the same Jesus of Nazareth.

A further 300 years passed and the space visitor came to the rocky coastline of Ireland. He found a group of men dressed in a common habit, standing ice-cold up to their necks in water, reciting psalms and praying with arms outstretched. Some of them went off in small boats across the waters to the Firth of Clyde, while others sat alone in caves. They were deeply concerned about personal holiness, showed heroic austerity and asceticism, and attached great importance to the festival of Easter. They were still using the same formula that he had heard the Christians hammering out at Nicea. But they were not nearly so concerned with theology or metaphysics, as with holiness.

Returning in 1840, our space visitor visited Exeter Hall in the Strand, and there found a vast and excited assembly of men and women listening to speeches about Africa. This group proposed to send missionaries with bibles and cotton seed to Africa. They too were concerned with holiness, but were appalled at the suggestion that it should be connected with standing in cold water, and they were entirely opposed to spending their lives isolated praying in caves. Instead, they were very active in social concerns, anxious to see the abolition of slavery, and keen to apply their beliefs to every part of life.

Finally, our space visitor returned in 1980, this time to Nigeria. There he found a white-robed group of Christians dancing and chanting on their way to church, warmly inviting others to come and experience the power of God, which they said was evident in their services. Individuals claimed to give particular messages from God, and to demonstrate healing. They still carried the same Book with them that was carried by the gentlemen who met in Exeter Hall, but they were not at all politically active.

Professor Walls posed the question: 'Is there anything coherent about the use of the name "Christian" by such diverse groups, or is it just fortuitous, or even misleading?' Perhaps you will keep this question in mind as we consider the diversity of religious belief and behaviour under the four headings I mentioned earlier, namely differences owing to personality factors, to chronological age, to denominational attachment and to prevailing but passing fashions.

Differences linked with personality factors and child-rearing practices

The basic question here is this: do religious people have a different kind of personality from non-religious people? And the additional question: do members of one religious denomination have personality characteristics distinguishable from those of another religious denomination? If we discover that there are such differences, the further question arises, which comes first, the religious affiliation producing personality differences, or personality differences predisposing the individual to attach himself to a particular religious group? It may also be that both the religious behaviour a person manifests and the religious group to which he attaches himself, as well as the personality he manifests, are the results of a further common factor, such as the child-rearing practices to which he has been subjected.

In the last twenty years, there have been a number of carefully conducted studies involving large numbers of people, which have looked into the correlations between religious beliefs, reported behaviour and measurable personality traits. The clearest of the results from these studies is that there is no simple relationship between religion and personality. For example, Professor Laurence Brown reported a study in 1962 involving 200 students, and found that the correlation between their religious beliefs and a standard measure of neuroticism was only 0.03, and between religious beliefs and extroversion was only 0.07.[6] I need hardly add that neither of these correlations was significant.

A much older study conducted by Brown and Lowe in 1951 involved almost 900 students and used a personality inventory familiar to psychologists, the Minnesota Multiphasic Personality Inventory.[7] They found no systematic relationship between personality profile and religious group membership. A fair assessment of these and many similar studies would be that the relation between religiosity and *general* personality traits is very weak. Nevertheless, it is worthwhile looking a little more closely at possible links between religion and *specialised* aspects of personality.

In a recent review Dr Benjamin Beit-Hallahmi, commenting on the search for the 'religious personality', pointed out that the layman expects the psychologist studying religion to come up with a psychological description of the 'typical religious person'. Thus, one is asked, what is the religious person like? How, if at all, is he different in personality from the irreligious person? He pointed out, however, as I have just done, that in the numerous studies that have tried to answer such questions and to produce the hoped-for global psychological profile of the religious person, the results have been disappointing. One reason for this is that it is difficult to define the truly religious person in any way that gains common acceptance. However, while there has been little success in discovering the typical personality profile of the religious person, there has been more limited success on a narrower front. For example, there is a fair amount of evidence that leads one to conclude that in Western society the merely *conventional* religious person is probably more authoritarian, dogmatic and suggestible than his non-religious counterpart.[8]

The question remains why the many attempts to relate personality profile to religiosity have been unsuccessful. One obvious reason is the complexity of variables and measurements that one is dealing with. Another is that the whole field of personality research has in recent years been in a state of upheaval. The most extreme position on this, which I mentioned in Chapter 1, is represented by the work of Mischel.[9] He went so far as to suggest that we should no longer look for personality traits that are stable from one situation to another, since these simply do not exist. Those taking less extreme positions have, nevertheless, emphasised an interactionist view, that behaviour is a function both of the traits on the personality profile and of the pressures from outside. The net result of all this has been a retreat to a position where one says that religious affiliation and religiosity remain useful labels for predicting *group* trends in behaviour, though not *individual* behaviour.

In order to illustrate how more *specialised* aspects of personality have been studied, we may look at an aspect of the religious personality that has received a good deal of attention, namely, the motivation of 'need-achievement' that I mentioned in my first chapter. The basic idea arises from the psychological elaboration of Max Weber's theory, put forward in 1904, that the Protestant ethic leads those who accept it, towards achievement, independence, and mastery of their environment. Such qualities became the stereotype of the Protestant as the one who works harder, saves money and does better economically. Weber saw this as coinciding with the rise of capitalism in a number of countries. In particular, he argued that the Reformers had emphasised that men would be judged *individually* on the basis of the use they had made of the talents they had received and of the extent to which they had fulfilled their calling. Moreover, according to this ethic, money once gained should not be spent on oneself. It was argued that this in turn led to a life characterised by hard work, disciplined asceticism,and determination to achieve as much as possible. It also led to the accumulation of wealth, because the spending of money on luxuries was frowned upon.

This theory was taken up and elaborated in 1961 by David McClelland, who offered a social psychological explanation of the link between Protestantism and capitalism. This is not the place to attempt an elaboration, for it is available in many places.[10] What McClelland did was to devise a psychological procedure for assessing the so-called 'motive to achieve'. In applying this instrument to rather small groups of Protestants, Jews and Catholics, he discovered that the Protestants and Jews scored higher on this need-achievement score than did Catholics. More recently, McClelland has shown that the Catholic/Protestant differences, which he first discovered in achievement motivation, could be accounted for by *social class factors* within the same society. More recently still, a large-scale study in the USA showed higher achievement scores among Catholics than among Protestants, with Jewish men scoring higher than either. When these findings were dissected according to age and income, it was discovered that it was the younger, lower-income Catholics with large families who were most likely to have high achievement scores, while high-income Catholics had lower scores. The general conclusion that seems to be accepted today is that in the USA, where most of this work has been done, there is no clear difference in achievement motivation between Catholics and Protestants, when socioeconomic and class factors are taken into account. So once again, the attempt to discover and establish a tight link between a personality trait and a religious affiliation has floundered.

Studies of religious conversion carried out by psychologists have frequently pointed to the importance of suggestibility as a predisposing factor. This is particularly the case when one is dealing with a sudden conversion. Some very old studies claimed to show that those who took a conservative religious position and who were also sudden converts were more suggestible than others. It would not be surprising if it were discovered that suggestion played an important part in conversion, and possibly a fairly significant part in sudden conversion. To talk thus loosely about suggestion is, however, to evade real problems that one faces in saying precisely what one means. As long ago as 1947, Professor Hans Eysenck pointed out that suggestibility is not just a single trait but is composed of a number of relatively independent elements.[11] He distinguised *primary* suggestibility, in which people carry out a motor action upon repeated suggestions by the experimenter, without any conscious participation in the event; *secondary* suggestibility in which people will perceive or remember what has been suggested; and *thirdly*, prestige or social suggestion in which people change the opinions that they had held when a prestige leader holds a different one.

Most books on psychology of religion now seem to agree that there is evidence that primary suggestibility is more in evidence in religious people. It has also been argued that it is more in evidence among members of revivalist and evangelical bodies. In some of the earlier revivals, many people showed signs of bodily movement, twitching and jerking, before finally collapsing. This view has been taken up in recent years, and has been re-examined and extended by William Sargant.[12] This is an example of *primary* suggestibility, and may be a particular trait of revivalist audiences when it occurs in the Christian context, although (as Sargant has shown) it is not restricted to the Christian context. The extensive study by Brown and Lowe in 1951, referred to above, tested large numbers of students on the Minnesota Multiphasic Personality Inventory and reported that a group of students of an extreme Protestant group who were at Bible Colleges scored higher on *hysteria*.

As regards *secondary* suggestibility, there is a little indirect evidence from a study of the effects of placebo treatment in hospitals. In one such study, it was claimed that those who responded to the placebo as bringing about relief of pain also reported a greater regularity of church attendance, and were often described as 'pillars of the Church'. A similar study carried out ten years later reported a correlation of 0.53 between placebo pain relief and religiosity. The *third* form of suggestibility, namely social suggestibility often due to prestige, is also said to be greater in religious people.

The question remains why religious people are more suggestible, if indeed they are. One possibility put forward by some, is that it is part of the teaching of the churches they attend that they should show humility, obedience and respect for authority. Others, however, believe that it is the other way around, namely that those who begin by being more suggestible are more likely to accept church teaching. Certainly, primary suggestibility that is linked with hysteria, has a *genetic* basis, and it is probably in this case that personality comes first and the response to various influences comes second. Social suggestibility, on the other hand, is more likely to be a product of social learning and could well be partly learned from the church environment. Here again, the results point to the dangers of making simplistic assertions of the kind that are too often made about religious people being more suggestible than others.

One other example must suffice for this discussion of personality factors and religion. It concerns the way in which a religious person handles his feelings of anger, and how this may be associated in turn with his feelings of guilt. It is sometimes asserted that the Protestant has a greater concern with sin than the Catholic, and that this is related to the relatively high suicide rate among Protestants, which in turn is a feature of their intrapunitive personality. That is, the Protestant directs his anger with himself inwards. By contrast, it is said that the Catholic directs his anger outwards; hence the fact that Catholics proscribe suicide, while showing a high crime rate.

There is some evidence, derived from using the physiological measure of King and Funkenstein, that those classified as religious conservatives are more likely to make the extrapunitive cardio-vascular response on their test.[13] This would agree with the most straightforward psychological testing done by Professor Laurence Brown, in which he gave the Rosensweig picture frustration test to a large group of Australian students.[14] He reported that the Catholics were more extrapunitive than the Protestants, and that the Prot-estant females were more intrapunitive than the Catholic females. Protestant males were also more intrapunitive. While not all the studies reported have confirmed these general findings, the evidence does suggest that Protestants have stronger guilt feelings and tend to direct their anger inwards towards themselves. What the correct explanation is remains a matter of opinion. It may be that Protestant teaching encourages feelings of guilt and discourages outward aggression. Or it may be that people with strong feelings are, in the first place, attracted to the Protestant message, with its emphasis on forgiveness and salvation. Certainly, some of the very oldest studies of conversion reported by Professor E. D. Starbuck[15] found that converts had strong guilt feelings before they were converted.

To conclude then on personality, we reiterate the unexciting conclusion that, on balance, the evidence suggests that religious beliefs and behaviour correlate very little with general personality traits. Where findings of significant correlations have occurred, they tend to be mainly with major ecclesiastical groupings, or with factors like child-rearing practices, occupational status or educational achievement. Moreover, the majority of such differences can probably be explained by class differences between the religious groups studied. Other differences may well be due to specific church teaching.

Two results remain, which do seem to relate personality mechanisms to religious activity. In the first place, there is the theory of a correlation between religiosity and suggestibility. And secondly, there seems to be a connection between guilt and the intrapunitiveness of Protestants, which may be due to the Church's teachings, but may also arise because guilty people or those who feel guilt are attracted by a particular exposition of the doctrines of salvation and forgiveness. In both these instances, it is difficult to know which is the chicken and which the egg.

Differences owing to the successive stages of the life cycle

How many, I wonder, of the tensions and conflicts that occur from time to time within the local church would be reduced if there could be a proper recognition of the ways in which the expression of religious affiliation varies across the life cycle from childhood through to old age? How many of the occasions when the older generation frown upon the religious expressions of the younger generation could be avoided if they would recognise the different functions of religious belief and behaviour at different ages? To illustrate, we will look briefly at some of the main features of religious attachment at different stages of the life cycle.

The development of religious thinking through childhood to

adolescence has been documented by several workers. Although in recent years the discussion that has gained the greatest publicity has been that based on the work of Professor Ronald Goldman,[16] it is well to remember that there were earlier studies such as those by Harms in 1944,[17] followed by the very profound and insightful discussion by Professor Gordon Allport.[18] Harms's study was an empirical one, in which several thousand children were asked to draw their idea of God and to give written or spoken comments with their drawing. While no statistical treatment was made of the data, Harms claimed that there were three clear stages apparent. From three to six years old there is what he called the 'fairy-tale' stage, in which God is frequently regarded in the same way as giants and dragons, but bigger and more powerful and often wearing flowing robes. From seven to eleven comes the 'realistic' stage, in which God is understood as a father and a real person, and during this time many orthodox ideas are accepted. Then from twelve upwards there emerges what is often called the 'individualistic' stage, in which a more personal religion develops, and interpretations of experience vary significantly from the mystical to the conventional.

Goldman's work was fitted into the framework of the earlier work of Professor Jean Piaget on the development of children's thinking. This work gained enormous publicity, and in some ways was too readily, uncritically and overenthusiastically accepted. Others, who have since worked more carefully on the same age ranges, have begun to add some necessary correctives to the story put forward by Goldman.

The next phase of religious development, labelled the *adolescent* phase, usually covers twelve to eighteen years of age. This, of course, is the time of life that has received the greatest attention, because it is so often the age of religious awakening. It is during this time that more professions of conversion occur than at any other time during the life cycle. Conversions away from childhood beliefs, as well as towards a Christian profession, occur at this time. This is not the place to discuss the many many studies done of religious conversion. Suffice it to say that the more we know about it, the more we realise the almost infinite variety of the predisposing factors leading to religious conversion. We also understand more and more that the way in which conversion is expressed is very dependent upon the situation in which the person concerned lives and in which he is introduced to religious ideas. It is as well to remember that adolescence is not only a time when young people express themselves forcibly and dogmatically about religious matters. It is also characteristic of this period that they adopt strong, clear and often extreme positions on a whole variety of issues – political, moral and economic as well as religious. If this were recognised a little more readily, perhaps people would be less likely to overreact to the enthusiasm shown by young people in their religious commitment, but instead accept and understand it.

The next period is young adulthood, from eighteen to thirty years. Most studies show that during this time there is a decline (often sharp) in religious activity, followed from thirty years old on by a fresh, continuous increase in religious activity.

The middle years of life, from thirty to sixty, have received less study by psychologists interested in the psychology of religion. In general, the evidence suggests that during these years there is an increase in active prayer, in acceptance of religious values, in belief in the importance of religion, and in a general interest in religion, although this is often not expressed in frequency of church attendance. Conversions of the most dramatic kind are less frequently reported after thirty years of age, although in some groups a second profound experience may be reported during this part of the life cycle. It is usually during this period that the middle-aged person comes to play a more active and perhaps more responsible role in the organisational aspects of church life. It is now also that the sorts of conflicts with the young that I mentioned earlier are most likely to occur. This is because middle-aged people do not always remember either their own earlier enthusiasm or that the religious enthusiasm of the contemporary younger generation should be accepted rather than frowned upon and censured.

From sixty years old onwards the evidence indicates a movement to traditional beliefs, with stability of faith and a beginning of disengagement from organised religion. The person who has worked most extensively on this is Professor David Moberg.[19] He believes that the research to date indicates fairly conclusively that ritualistic behaviour outside the home, of a religious kind, tends to diminish with increasing age, but that at the same time religious attitudes and feelings increase among those people who have some form of acknowledged religion. Thus, religion as a set of external rituals, which are indulged in outside the home, steadily drops off in old age, but the internal personal response concerned with a man's relationship with God apparently increases among older religious people. In this sense, both disengagement from and re-engagement with religion are typical of old age. Some people have even suggested that this is a distinction that may be related to the age-old contrast between faith and work. They suggest that many of the objective practices that they define as works of religion have become increasingly difficult to perform in old age, as the body and mind gradually show the effects of ageing. Yet at the same time, the spirit of the religious person remains alive, and his beliefs and feelings become ever more intense, even though his institutional attachments diminish.

Differences related to denominational attachment

Both believers and unbelievers are familiar with the wide range of differences between Christian denominations. They are an object lesson in how those who claim to share a common core of belief nevertheless express them in a wide variety of ways, when it comes to religious practices both personal and corporate. Thus the manner of meeting, the extent and nature of the rituals used, the degree of congregational involvement, the ways in which religious experiences are typically described – all this gives ample evidence both of a common core and of differences of expression. That essentially similar experiences are described so differently is a good example of a general point made earlier, namely, the selective nature of perceiving, thinking, feeling and remembering. Again, the question is raised as to which comes first. Does the temperament precede the decision to affiliate with a particular religious group? Or is it the effect of early environment that predisposes individuals to join particular religious denominations or groups?

For example, do those individuals who are naturally more thoughtful select the more staid and reflective ways in which their worship may be expressed? Do the introverts look for ministry that emphasises the inner life? Do the extroverts look for a ministry that minimises introspection and avoids unnecessary soul-searching? Each of us, I suspect, is inclined to say that we, for our part, have deliberately selected the way we worship and the denomination we have joined, whereas others have been constrained by developmental and environmental forces. Perhaps it would be more helpful if we saw these same forces acting upon ourselves as upon others. At the same time, we cannot help feeling, as we examine some of the extremes, that temperament and personality *do* play an important part. Who for example can read the life of William Cowper,[20] remember his episodes of depression, and sing his great hymns, without feeling that his religious expression was reflecting his intrinsic melancholic personality?

It is at this point that it becomes doubly important to recognise how difficult it is to see ourselves as others see us. Sometimes we can be helped in doing this by looking at more extreme groups. I recently read of the attempt of a Professor of Religion at a small college in Tennessee, who used what he called the method of contrast and excessive representation in order to bring home to some of his students aspects of their own behaviour that otherwise they found difficult to countenance. His students came from the most fundamentalist, conservative and anti-intellectual groups of the so-called 'Bible Belt'. Within the same town there were two small cults who engaged in the handling of poisonous snakes as part of their normal worship and ritual. By getting his students to visit these groups at worship, to study their behaviour, to note their socioeconomic class, and observe carefully all that took place, they became more reflective about whether similar forces might not to some extent be at work in their own religious group, and the way they themselves expressed their religious behaviour. Perhaps this applies to all of us. We all find it difficult to be critically reflective about our own feelings, attachments and behaviour. Perhaps were we more so, we would be more ready to recognise the freedom of others to express their beliefs and worship in a different way.

Differences that reflect changing religious movements

At the beginning of this chapter, I referred to the provocative lecture by Professor Andrew Walls, and how it underlined the way in which an authentic commitment to the central tenets of the Christian faith can manifest itself in widely different ways. As we looked at the Jewish Christians in Jerusalem in the first century, at the participants in the Council of Nicea in AD 325, at the monks in Ireland in AD 600, at the beginnings of the missionary outreach in Britain, and at contemporary Christianity in West Africa, we had to accept that, though widely different in the external accompaniments, there was nevertheless an underlying continuity.

Anyone who is even mildly observant must notice a similar variety of Christian expression around us today, many of which claim to represent authentic Christian experience and behaviour. In trying to understand this, a number of different attitudes may be taken. There are, in the first place, those who are frankly amazed at what is claimed to be authentically Christian within another culture, while at the same time they fail to recognise some of the same features embedded within their own particular religious culture. The students in Tennessee mentioned above are an example of this. Another reaction is to generalise from one's own particular experience and culture and to believe that this must be the norm for all cultures and contexts. Thirdly, there is the most obvious reaction of all, namely that as an outside observer one completely misinterprets the behaviour concerned because one has not understood the context within which it occurs. I came across such an instance only recently. A Jewish scholar pointed out that it should not surprise psychologists studying the beliefs, experiences and behaviours of orthodox Jews to discover that they simply do *not* know what is being talked about when they are asked about religious experiences in everyday life. For them, so he asserted, they can only recognise religious experiences within the institutional context, that is, within the synagogue. It is therefore not surprising, so he claimed, that they give no reports of religious experience in relation, for example, to nature, as is so often done in the West. It was Freud himself who said, 'We Jews have an easier time having no mystical experience'. On the same occasion, a devout Jewish lady responded by saying that in her experience, Jewish women in London *do* report religious experiences in everyday life, not in respect to nature, nor in terms of ecstatic mysticism, but rather as focused on a practical commandment and its daily observance.

Finally, I must comment briefly on some of the more newsworthy contemporary trends, in which the freedom to differ often seems to raise the greatest controversy and strength of feeling. The obvious candidate is 'glossolalia'. I do not claim to be an expert on this topic. I might add in parenthesis that I doubt if many who speak about it are. It is, however, a good example, since it is a form of behaviour and experience usually found in the religious context where individuals show marked differences from others and where they are judged on the basis of this different behaviour.

Perhaps what is not sufficiently realised is that it is a phenomenon that has occurred for a very long time. In 1956 L. Carlyle-May of Harvard University published a review paper on glossolalia in the *American Anthropologist*.[21] He traced its history both in the Christian religion and in non-Christian religions. He referred to Heroditus' account of the inspired priests in Greece who suddenly spoke in a barbarian language, and to Virgil in the Aeneid who wrote of a sibyl who spoke strangely while possessed. The Old Testament alludes to a form of ecstatic behaviour similar to glossolalia, and others refer to accounts as far back as 853 BC, where prophets appear to have entered into ecstatic states. Certainly, in ancient Egypt some of the necromancers uttered such strange formulae. The more mysterious and incomprehensible the formulae were, the greater their power was thought to be. An example of glossolalia in the later Han dynasty (AD 196) indicated the antiquity of the phenomenon in China. Phenomena of this kind have occurred in widely different parts of the Western world and occasionally outside the Western world. This is not the place to go into the fine distinctions that have been made between different types of glossolalia. Suffice it to say that the evidence is clear enough that 'speaking in tongues' and similar behaviour have occurred in widely variegated forms and in widespread contexts. The psychological explanations given for such phenomena vary within the different religions. The religious explanations include that of Buddhism and of the Dansing religion of Japan, the former being based on the idea of transmigration of souls, the latter upon specific spirits possessing the glossolalist. Generally speaking, the Christian interpretation is that 'tongues' is a gift of God. It is a spiritual *charisma*, along with such other gifts as prophecy, healing, performing miracles and interpretation of tongues. It is also suggested that it is usually found in religions that are tolerant of highly emotional individualistic behaviour, such as we find in medicine men and their assistants. On the whole, however, glossolalia occurs infrequently in both Christian and non-Christian religions. Whatever else we may say, speaking in tongues is widespread in its occurrence and variation. From a psychological point of view, it has been pointed out that the most impressive features are the depersonalised and automatic aspects of tongue speaking, the emphasis on being externally controlled, and the different reactions one finds to these phenomena.[22]

Perhaps the other contemporary phenomenon on which I should comment is that of the emergence of small groups of communally organised adherents to new religions, especially in the USA and in some parts of Europe. These have received intense and sustained study in recent years by Professor James Richardson and others.[23] As a result, in North America certain profiles have emerged to characterise the adherents of such groups. There seems to be general agreement that in most of the groups studied in the USA the special characteristics of members are that they tend to be male, single, upper class, often with a history of drug addiction, alcoholism, and excessive and/or perverted sexual behaviour. Many of them have been located in socially affluent groups before moving into these particular groups, and have been well educated. Not infrequently, they have caused grief and consternation among their families by joining such groups, and yet (a point that has to be made to avoid misjudgments) many of them change from being dependency-prone personalities. The actual figures show that whereas beforehand 97 per cent were on drugs, 91 per cent on alcohol and 76 per cent on tobacco, these percentages dropped to zero dependency afterwards. There certainly seems to be evidence of good rehabilitation by these people, and of dramatic change in their sexual activity. What also has to be stated, although it should be obvious, is that because by adhering to such groups quite marked beneficial changes in personality state and in general behaviour are witnessed, this in itself does not say anything one way or the other about the truth or falsehood of the beliefs held. These must be judged on the appropriate evidence in each case. What needs to be said is that the wholesale denigration of such groups does not do justice to the facts, and that in not a few cases they have performed a positive therapeutic function.

Conclusion: the centrality of Christ

It will, I hope, be evident by now that there are vast differences in religious beliefs, experience and behaviour. This fact should alert us to the temptation to focus on local, cultural, transient and ultimately superficial aspects, and to confer upon them a primacy and finality that they do not deserve.

Several times I have raised the question, as we have looked at the wide variety of expressions of religious beliefs and behaviour, is there an authentic Christian mark and, if so, what is it? I have pointed out that even this question must be approached with caution because, as we look at Scripture, we are prone to read it through the particular spectacles that we have acquired through *our own* early experiences, background and ecclesiastical and social groupings. In consequence, we are prone to the ubiquitous tendency of selective perceiving, selective thinking and selective remembering. It is at this point that a responsible approach to the interpretation of Scripture is so important. The task of Christian biblical hermeneutics is to enable us in our cultural context and our personal and social constraints to hear God's word speaking today through the words that were spoken or written in cultures and contexts very different from our own. Clearly we do not have time to elaborate this now.

I want to close, however, by pointing you to one paragraph of the New Testament that I believe points to the essential continuity between Christians of all ages, cultures and traditions. I invite you to see whether or not you share my view that it encapsulates the authentic Christian core, which must be evident in any individual or group claiming to be Christian in the biblical sense.

The common feature found in all the groups visited by Professor Walls's hypothetical space visitor was that without exception they acknowledged *the supremacy and the sufficiency of Christ*. This is summarised very clearly in the first chapter of the apostle Paul's letter to the Christians at Colossae. My quotations are from the New English Bible, First, *Jesus Christ is supreme in who he is*. 'He is the image of the invisible God' (v. 15) (RSV). In other words, if you want to know what God is like, look at Jesus. Again, 'In him the complete being of God by God's own choice came to dwell' (v. 19). And again, 'It is in Christ that the complete being of the Godhead dwells embodied' (2.9). Thus, Jesus is Lord because of his very nature. It is because of who he is that the other theme of this epistle, the other authentic mark I mentioned, is seen so clearly, namely *the sufficiency of Christ*. At the risk of using jargon, it is because Christ is supreme by his very nature that he is a sufficient saviour. It is in him that 'our release is secured and our sins forgiven' (1.14). Then the apostle hurries on to tell us, secondly, that Christ is *supreme in creation*: 'In him everything in heaven and on earth was created . . . the whole universe has been created through him and for him' (v. 16). Christ is Lord of creation, the creator and upholder of all that is. And thirdly, Jesus Christ is also supreme as *Lord of the Church*. He is 'the head of the body, the Church. He is its origin, the first to return from the dead, to be in all things alone supreme' (v. 18).

Here then is the perspective from which to view our differences. True unity and effective endeavour in the body of Christ will not come merely by a reorganisation of its structures, nor by the uniformity of its members, but by a renewed obedience within our diversity to the same divine Head. This is the continuity that we have with the Jerusalem Christians of AD 37, the Greek Christians of Nicea, the monks in Ireland, the eighteenth-century Christians and our contemporary African brethren. By that same grace we have been enabled to confess Jesus as Lord, Lord by virtue of his nature, Lord of creation, Lord of the Church, supreme and all-sufficient.

If this is the authentic core of Christian belief, there is within this same letter the authentic mark of Christian behaviour. As so often, the apostle Paul rushes on from lofty theological truths to their practical outworking. 'You', he says in the very next verses, 'were estranged from God', 'you were his enemies in heart and mind', 'but now . . . God has reconciled you to himself', 'only you must continue in the faith' (v. 21–3). Certainly the apostle had no doubt whatever about what the lordship of Christ involves in behavioural terms for every authentic Christian. It means that we must, as he writes later in the letter (3:12, 13 and 14), 'put on the garments that suit God's chosen people, his own, his beloved'. What are these garments? 'Compassion, kindness, humility, gentleness, patience. Be forbearing with one another and forgiving when any of you has cause for complaint: you must forgive as the Lord forgave you. To crown all, there must be love, to bind all together and complete the whole.' This surely encapsulates the authentic mark that must be evident amid all our Christian diversity. It is *the acknowledgment that Jesus is Lord, evidenced by the love that binds all together and completes the whole.*

Notes

1. William Sargant, *Battle for the Mind* (Heinemann, London, 1957).
2. William Sargant, *The Mind Possessed* (Heinemann, London, 1973).
3. Sigmund Freud, *The Future of an Illusion* (Hogarth Press, London, 1934).
4. M. A. Jeeves, *Psychology and Christianity – The View Both Ways* (IVP, Leicester, 1976).
5. Andrew Walls, 'The Gospel as the Prisoner and Liberator of Culture', *Faith and Thought;* vol. 108, nos 1 and 2 (1981), pp. 39–52.
6. L. B. Brown, 'A Study of Religious Belief', *British Journal of Psychology,* vol. 53 (1962), pp. 259–72.
7. D. G. Brown and W. L. Lowe, 'Religious Beliefs and Personality Characteristics of College Students', *Journal of Social Psychology,* vol. 33 (1951), pp. 103–29.
8. M. Argyle and B. Beit-Hallahmi, *The Social Psychology of Religion* (Routledge & Kegan Paul, London, 1975).
9. W. Mischel, *Personality Assessment* (Wiley, 1968).
10. D. C. McClelland, J. S. Atkinson, R. A. Clark and E. L. Lowell, *The Achievement Motive* (Appleton-Century-Crofts, New York, 1953).
11. H. J. Eysenck, *Dimensions of Personality* (Routledge & Kegan Paul, London, 1947).
12. Sargant, *Battle for the Mind,* op. cit.
13. S. H. King and D. H. Funkenstein, 'Religious Practice and Cardiovascular Reactions During Stress', *Journal of Abnormal and Social Psychology,* vol. 55 (1957), pp. 135–7.
14. L. B. Brown, 'Aggression and Denominational Membership', *British Journal of Social and Clinical Psychology,* vol. 4 (1965), pp. 175–8.
15. E. D. Starbuck, *The Psychology of Religion* (Walter Scott, London, 1899).
16. R. J. Goldman, *Religious Thinking from Childhood to Adolescence* (Routledge & Kegan Paul, London, 1964).
17. E. Harms, 'The Development of Religious Experience in Children', *American Journal of Sociology,* vol. 50 (1944), pp. 112–22.
18. G. W. Allport, *The Individual and His Religion* (Macmillan, New York, 1950).
19. For example, D. O. Moberg, 'Religiosity in Old Age', *Gerontologist,* vol. 5 (1965), pp. 78–87.
20. Lord David Cecil, *The Stricken Deer* (Constable, London, 1929).

21. L. Carlyle-May, *American Anthropologist*, vol. 58 (1956), pp. 75–96.
22. The definition given of glossolalia by W. J. Samarin in his publications is 'a meaningless but phonologically structured human utterance believed by the speaker to be a real language but bearing no systematic resemblance to any natural language, living or dead'.
23. For example, James T. Richardson, 'Conversion, Brainwashing and Deprogramming', *Center Magazine*, vol. 15, no. 2 (1982), pp. 18–24; James T. Richardson, R. B. Simmonds and M. Harder, 'Thought Reform and the Jesus Movement', *Youth Society*, vol. 4 (1972), pp. 185–200.

5: Sex

R. J. Berry

Some years ago I invited a very distinguished scientist to teach my students on the subject 'What is sex?' He spoke for an hour and a half on the biological basis for two sexes, and the forces affecting their maintenance. The scientist concerned is a good lecturer and a frequent broadcaster; his talk was clear and logical. Some months later I set a straightforward three-word question in the final exam for the same students, 'What is sex?' Not one attempted it. For a group of normal students in biology to avoid such an apparently simple question shows how complicated the subject really is.

A flavour of its complexity comes from recognising that we have to divide sex *per se* into chromosomal, hormonal and behavioural sex. Our chromosomal sex is determined at fertilisation (if we have a Y chromosome we are genetically male; if we have no Y chromosome, we are female). Differentiation into male and female depends on hormones secreted during early development, and can be affected by the embryo's capacity to produce and also to respond to specific hormones, and to some extent to the mother's chemistry (in particular whether she is taking certain drugs). And a child forms its behaviour by modelling himself or herself on the training and expectation of the society in which he or she is reared. (If someone is brought up as the 'wrong' sex owing to having ambiguous genitalia at birth, or to parental desires for a boy or a girl, conflicts may develop at puberty when secondary sexual characteristics develop; in extreme cases 'sex change surgery' may have to be carried out.)

Even this three fold separation of the factors leading to gender is incomplete, but it serves as an introduction to two points:

1. Sex is not *simply* determined by the chance of whether a male-determining or a female-determining sperm reaches an ovum first.

The person we are depends on interactions between our genetical constitution and a large number of successive environments both before and after birth. This is a specific example of the general conclusion in my previous chapter, that adult characteristics (and clearly sex is a very important characteristic) are not dependent on genes alone. Or, in other words, our bodies and our behaviour are not automatically produced by a genetic blueprint in our chromosomes. Furthermore, it is obviously inadequate to think of sex as nothing but the consequence of chromosomes, hormones or behaviour. Although we may have to concentrate on one of these elements in dealing with a particular problem, which might relate to appearance (hairy women, men with breasts, etc.), infertility, aggressiveness, or social psychology, yet in general we have to approach sex as a hierarchy of different processes. The physicist Mach's definition of science as 'a minimal problem consisting of the completest presentation of facts with the least possible expenditure of thought' has too often produced a blinkered naivety because the facts considered have not been 'the completest'. We cannot reduce sex to nothing more than (say) steroid chemistry.[1] Sexual differentiation illustrates the dangers of the two half-truths of determinism and reductionism introduced in Chapter 1 by Malcolm Jeeves and developed by me in Chapter 2.

2. There has been a tendency in recent years to regard the sexes as almost interchangeable: with the exception of child-bearing, everything a man does is capable of being done by a woman, and *vice versa*. Independent of this, although often championed by the same people, is the argument that maleness and femaleness are extremes of a continuum, and that any person may remain exclusively at one extreme throughout his or her life, or may show behaviour characteristic of the other sex to a greater or lesser extent, or for a longer or shorter period.

The assumed male-female continuum received apparent support from the scale of 'sexual preference' devised by Alfred Kinsey.[2] According to the responses of 5,300 volunteer males (Kinsey's subjects in both his major studies on men (1948) and women (1953) did not involve a random sample of the population), Kinsey arranged everyone on a seven-point scale, ranging from exclusively heterosexual (K-0) to exclusively homosexual (K-6); the mid-point (K-3) represented equal hetero- and homo- sexual orientation.

Kinsey claimed that his results proved there was no such thing as normality or abnormality in sex. He found that 4–5 per cent of his American males and 2 per cent of American females were exclusively homosexual (K-6) throughout their lives; that 37 per cent of the males had had some homosexual experience at some stage during their life; and that 19 per cent of women had had 'physical contact intended to be erotic' with another female by the age of forty. While showing that homosexual behaviour was far commoner than had previously been accepted, it ought to be clear from the arguments in Chapter 2 that such behaviour does not necessarily *prove* an underlying genetic determination. We shall return to the question of genetics and homosexuality later. But it must be emphasised here that the Kinsey figures depend on homosexual periods of activity; mathematically they do not indicate a sexual continuum, nor are they evidence that every individual has a fixed heterosexual or homosexual predisposition.

Sociobiology

The main subject of this chapter is sexual determination and sexual behaviour, and how they are connected. Before we consider some examples of this, it is worth digressing to consider the interest and possible importance of the burgeoning science of sociobiology, which has been claimed to provide a coherent explanation of behaviour ethics. Peter Singer has written:

> Sociobiology . . . enables us to see ethics as a mode of human reasoning which develops in a group context . . . so ethics loses its air of mystery. Its principles are not laws written up in Heaven. Nor are they absolute truths about the universe, known by intuition. The principles of ethics come from our own nature as social, reasoning beings.[3]

The term sociobiology was coined by a behavioural geneticist, John P. Scott in 1946. He defined it as 'an interdisciplinary science which lies between the fields of biology (particularly ecology and physiology) and psychology and sociology'. It can therefore be said to deal with precisely the same subjects as this book, with the exception that we have firmly added theology!

Sociobiology acquired a firm theoretical base with the studies of W. D. Hamilton on 'inclusive fitness' and J. Maynard Smith on 'kin selection'. They showed that under certain specified conditions, genes for traits which may be detrimental to their possessor may spread in a population through natural selection. In other words, a characteristic such as altruism may be selected in the same way as (for example) inherited resistance to a disease. (The human blood groups are generally assumed to have acquired different frequencies in different populations because of the differing susceptibility of some types to the epidemic diseases of the past).

Traditionally, biologists have been unable to explain why moral virtues should evolve, since they might be expected to hinder their possessors in the struggle for existence. Charles Darwin himself had this dilemma:

> It is extremely doubtful whether the offspring of the more sympathetic and benevolent parents, or of those who were the most faithful to their comrades, would be reared in greater numbers than the children of selfish and treacherous parents belonging to the same tribe. He who was ready to sacrifice his life, as many a savage has been, rather than betray his comrades, would often leave no offspring to inherit his noble nature. The bravest men, who were always willing to come to the front in war, and who freely risked their lives for others, would on an average perish in larger numbers than other men. Therefore it hardly seems probable then the number of men gifted with such virtues, or the standard of their excellence, could be increased through natural selection, that is, by the survival of the fittest.[4]

Fifty years ago, J. B. S. Haldane pointed out that if the unselfishness (even to the point of self-sacrifice) of an individual had an inherited basis, and if it helped his near relatives, then 'altruistic genes' would be selected in families; there could be situations where co-operation (i.e. unselfishness) is an advantage to a group of relatives. Haldane's argument was formalised in 1964 by W. D. Hamilton[5] by the concept of 'inclusive fitness' or (as it has since become known) 'kin selection'.

The 1950s and 1960s saw much interest in biology and behaviour, shown in the writing of Konrad Lorenz, Niko Tinbergen, Wynne-Edwards, Robert Ardrey, and Desmond Morris, and expressed in such television series as David Attenborough's *Life on Earth*. Sociobiology entered common language with the publication in 1975 of a book called *Sociobiology: The New Synthesis*[6] by Edward Wilson, a distinguished entomologist who has spent many years studying social insects (ants, termites, bees, etc.). Wilson ranged widely through the animal kingdom, concluding with a chapter entitled 'Man: From Sociobiology to Sociology', where he applied the conclusions from other animals about genes and behaviour to man. He later expanded this chapter into a book called *On Human Nature*.[7] In this Wilson expounds sociobiology as providing a biological underpinning for sociology: 'Biology is the key to human nature, and social scientists cannot afford to ignore its rapidly tightening principles.' Wilson has been attacked by both sociologists and socialists, who see his ideas as contrary to their dreams of improving society by manipulating the environment.[8] We are not concerned with these here: they are inspired more by political preconceptions than by science; what we are concerned with is to examine the explicit suggestions that Wilson makes about sex, and in particular homosexuality.

The selfish gene

Before we return to sex, however, it is necessary to note that Wilson's ideas depend on determinism. He recognises this himself ('On its interpretation depends the entire relation between biology and social sciences'), and he is much less dogmatic than many of his accusers. For example, 'Human genes prescribe the *capacity* to develop a certain array of traits. In some categories of behaviour the array is limited and the outcome can be altered only by strenuous training – if ever. In others the array is vast and the outcome easily influenced.' Wilson illustrates this point by considering left and right handedness, the effect of certain mutant genes such as phenyl-ketonuria on overall intelligence, and schizophrenia.

The ease with which we think of behaviour as being invariable (or deterministic) if it has an inherited base, is well illustrated by Richard Dawkins's *The Selfish Gene*.[9] Dawkins specifically invokes non-genetic elements ('memes') as the carriers of culture, and in so doing is following directly in the paths of Julian Huxley who saw us as now in a phase of psychosocial evolution and of C. H. Waddington who wrote about our sociogenetic evolution. But in linking genes with behaviour, Dawkins invokes an assumption of irrevocably fixed behaviours like that in many animals (e.g. courtship in insects or nest-building in birds). However, he also recognises two sorts of altruism, a biological one originating through kin selection, and one arising elsewhere (although from where he does not specify). In *The Selfish Gene* he wrote:

> If you wish, as I do, to build a society in which individuals co-operate generously and unselfishly towards a common good, you can expect little help from biological nature. Let us try to *teach* [my italics] generosity and altruism, because we are born selfish.

And:

> It is possible that yet another unique quality of man is a capacity for genuine, disinterested, true altruism. . . . We have the power to defy the selfish genes of our birth and, if necessary, the selfish memes of our indoctrination. We can even discuss ways of deliberately cultivating and nurturing pure, disinterested altruism – something that has no place in nature.

Sociobiology and sociobiologists have generated considerable controversy in the past decade, and some useful research. Evangelical Christians have been wary of their ideas, suspecting that any acknowledgment that genes influence behaviour somehow reduces our capability for behavioural choice and hence our accountability (to God or man). This is not an unreasonable reaction, but it cannot be upheld once we analyse what determinism means in the context. In Chapter 2 I argued that our understanding of the nature of life must influence our attitudes towards it. Here I draw exactly the same inference: we must examine the determinants of behaviour (including sexual behaviour), and not espouse an ethic that has little to do with reality. T. H. Huxley fully recognised this in reviling the liberal theologians of his time; it is good for once to count him among the angels:

> It is the secret of the superiority of the best theological teachers

to the majority of their opponents, that they substantially recognise the realities of things, however strange the forms in which they clothe their conceptions. The doctrines of predestination; of original sin; of the primacy of Satan in this world, appear to me to be vastly nearer the truth than the 'liberal' popular illusions that babies are all born good and that the example of a corrupt society is responsible for their failure to remain so; that it is given to everybody to reach the ethical ideal if he will only try.[10]

Sexual deviation

One clear fact that emerged from Kinsey's studies is that sexual activity is far more common than had previously been assumed. The unmarried males aged between sixteen and fifty in Kinsey's sample managed an average of 3.4 'sexual outlets' per week (including masturbation, natural emission, hetero- and homosexual activity, and bestiality), 'demonstrating the failure of the attempt to impose complete abstinence. . . . This is evidence of the ineffectiveness of social restrictions, and of the imperativeness of the biologic demand.'[11] Adolescent American females only have 20 per cent of the sexual activity of the male. Kinsey[12] deplored this, and commended premarital sex as a necessary recipe for happiness in marriage (which he equated with the frequency of orgasm).

The inferences made by Kinsey (and many others) about sexual behaviour have been fairly universally condemned by Christians, who have taken their stand on a supposed norm derived from natural law and Bible teaching (usually based on a particular interpretation of Paul's exposition in Romans 1.26,27). But can this attitude be upheld in the face of the amount[13] and variety of sexual activity that clearly goes on (even if we query the absolute level of this activity)?

It is quite impossible to survey the whole range of sexual behaviour in a single chapter. In some ways it is difficult to define precisely where normality ends and abnormality begins. Although most people would agree with the behaviours listed as abnormal by the psychiatrist Anthony Storr in his book *Sexual Deviation* (sado-masochism, fetishism, transvestism, homosexuality, exhibitionism, frotteurism, voyeurism, bestiality, paedophilia), there are many who would dissent from one or more of the list. Storr himself suggests that the anomalies he describes might be best regarded as indicators of emotional immaturity. He points out that:

> although it may be impossible to define normality in sexual behaviour even within the confines of a single society, there do exist standards in terms of which it is impossible to make comparative appraisals. One such standard is that of emotional maturity. The emphasis on this varies from writer to writer, but there is so much agreement on what constitutes maturity that the concept provides a useful yardstick against which to measure deviation. . . . If we are people who are unable fully to emerge from childhood, our childishness will inevitably manifest itself in our sexual behaviour; and a sexual deviation can generally be understood in terms of the persistence of a childish kind of relation to the other person, or else an attempt to overcome such a relation and so reach a greater degree of adult freedom.[14 15]

Storr's confidence that an understanding of emotional maturity is common ground is debatable. Notwithstanding, it accords with the biblical description of a mature, wise man. (Jas. 1.5–8; 1 Tim. 3.5, 6; Heb. 5.14; etc.) and provides a valuable basis of aim. An acid test for this interpretation is provided by homosexuality. Western societies have tended to abhor and outlaw homsexuality (with the possible exception of the latter days of the Graeco-Roman Empire) basing themselves on the apparently clear condemnation of homosexual practice in the Bible (at Sodom and at Gibeah: Gen. 19, Judg. 19; in the Levitical law: Lev. 18.22, 20.13; and by Paul in the New Testament: Rom. 1.27, 1 Cor. 6.9,10; and 1 Tim. 1.9,10).[16] Recent apologists, however, (most importantly Sherwin Bailey)[17] have argued that the real sin in the Old Testament stories was a violation of the duty of hospitality to strangers, and that in the New Testament we should distinguish between *perversion* (involving a licentious search for thrills) and *inversion* (a constitutional and therefore, it is maintained, a 'natural' preference for the same sex felt by exclusive homosexuals). Somewhat similarly, a recent paper by Barnabas Lindars on *The Use of Scripture*[18] claimed that:

> Paul's attitude to homosexuality is a standard Jewish position of the time, and owes nothing to his newly found Christian faith. He uses it because he needs an example of false worship leading

> to depravity, and he can take it for granted that this example will be common ground between him and his readers (Jewish Christians or Gentile converts influenced by Jewish ethics).

Interpretations by such as Bailey and Lindars are at best debatable and at worst casuistical special pleading, but they illustrate the possibility of an apologetic for homosexuality from those who accept Christian teaching. This is not the place to join the debate about exegesis.[19] Rather, I want to enter the debate from the other end and ask what produces a homosexual disposition, to what extent we can regard it as a normal variant of sexual development, and whether this renders the condition and its expression in homosexual behaviour morally acceptable.

Is homosexuality a matter for concern?

It is difficult to achieve a balanced perspective on homosexuality. If the frequently quoted figure of about one in every fifteen to twenty people having a homosexual predisposition is right, it means that enormous numbers of homosexuals exist, all of whom experience personal stresses in a predominantly and avowedly heterosexual society. It is clearly very important to decide whether homosexuality is an evil, an illness, or a legitimate expression of sexuality. But such an analysis is complicated by pressure groups ranging from a commercial vested interest in 'gays' to the irrationalities of 'queer-bashers', with an uneasy middle ground dotted with liberal groups such as those pressing for a 'Charter for Homosexual Rights' on the ground that 'fear or hatred of homosexuals is a social evil akin to anti-semitism, racism, slavery and with the same evil consequences. It harms both the victimised individuals, and the society which tolerates it.'

In asking questions about homosexuality, I have purposely distanced myself from pastoral concerns; my aim in the discussion that follows belongs wholly to the context of a general discussion of problems raised by treating sex in a deterministic or reductionist way, and as part of the theme of this book. In brief, are we 'free to differ' in our sexual behaviour?[20]

The causes of homosexuality

There is a strong tradition, assumed by many and explicit in the Thomist version of natural law, that 'natural' characteristics are not candidates for ethical argument. The official Roman Catholic position on contraception and abortion reflects this attitude. It begs the question of what is 'natural'; indeed, it often blurs the problem by equating naturalness with inherited constitution. This assumption could be maintained when most people were believed to be genetically uniform at most of their gene-loci; but it becomes increasingly difficult as the implications of intra- and inter-population variation are worked out. Nevertheless, it is implied in frequently expressed phrases such as 'he couldn't help it; he's made that way'. In Chapter 2, I touched on the dilemma for Christians as to whether they should override (or subjugate) their genetic urges, and pointed out that Christians tend to have a different attitude from the secular world about this. This problem comes up in an acute form with homosexuality, and therefore a key question is whether a homosexual disposition is innate or acquired.

As Storr says in *Sexual Deviation* (pp 82, 83):

> all homosexuals have a vested interest in affirming that their condition is an inborn abnormality rather than the result of circumstances, for any other explanation is bound to imply criticism either of themselves or of their families, and usually of both. If the ability to have fully satisfying relations with the opposite sex is accepted as one criterion of emotional maturity, it follows that to be homosexual is to be immature; and, however much one may argue that such a condition is a result of circumstances outside the control of the individual, a failure to surmount these circumstances is implied, which reflects upon the person concerned in a way which a purely genetic explanation does not. If our faults can be attributed to our stars or our chromosomes, we do not feel as responsible for them as we do for those which can be attributed to the errors of our parents, and to our difficulties in overcoming these errors.

The question of inheritance occurs repeatedly in writings by homosexuals themselves. For example, Hirschfield in *Encyclopaedia Sexualis*[21] claimed:

> That the homosexual urge is not acquired but inborn is apparent from the phenomenon of its tenacity. Were it caused by external influences, it would be necessary to assume that it would yield to extraneous influences. In such a case, it would be possible not only for the heterosexual individual to become homosexual, but also for a homosexual to become heterosexual. Both assumptions are at variance with the results of abundant experience. It is certain, on the other hand, that men and women of extraordinary strong character and will-power were unable to change the direction of their sex urge in spite of great effort.

Kinsey listed fourteen different factors that at one time or another have been suggested as producing homosexuality. These can be simplified to four, one of which is genetic; the other three are hormonal, social, and psychodynamic.

As far as genetic causation is concerned, a much-quoted study by Kallman[22] found that both members in every one of forty pairs of identical twins (formed by the splitting of a single fertilised egg, so that they share exactly the same set of genes) were avowed homosexuals, whereas only 50 per cent of a series of non-identical twins were concordant. However, this finding was an incidental result of a major study of mental disease, and thirty of the forty pairs of identical twins were badly schizoid. The study was carried out without personal interviews, and it would be foolish to assume a high genetic component on the basis of this study alone. The Maudsley Hospital twin register recorded the incidence of homosexuality to be 6.1 per cent in eighty-two identical twin pairs and 7.2 per cent in ninety-seven non-identical pairs, and other workers have reported many identical twin pairs discordant for homosexuality. Indeed, twin studies for homosexuality illustrate the general problem of separating inherited from environmental factors. Twins are more likely to copy each other than ordinary sibs, and the conventional technique of assuming that differences in incidence or concordance between identical and non-identical twins indicate the extent of genetical involvement in a condition tends to be inefficient. There are several reports of high numbers of homosexuals in particular families; these do not give any information about the influence (or lack of it) of genetical factors.[23]

Neither single gene nor chromosome anomalies seem to determine homosexuality. Although chromosomal mutations involving the X or Y sex chromosomes may affect sexual development and behaviour, their effect is always to reduce sex drive. Likewise, there are no examples of segregation in families that would be produced by single gene determination. Although a degree of genetic involvement in the causation of homosexuality cannot be ruled out, there are no grounds for claiming that genes are particularly important.

However, the conclusion from one approach is interesting and may be important. Homosexuals are often portrayed as female-like in build if male, or masculine if female. Before techniques for chromosome analysis were developed, it was sometimes suggested that homosexuals were either hermaphrodites or 'intersexual'. We can now be much more definite about these conditions. Hermaphrodites have both male and female gonads, and are often a mosaic of different genetic cell types, while intersexuality represents a failure of the gonads to secrete the appropriate hormones and produce secondary sexual characteristics (it is most commonly chromosomally determined). But the earlier misapprehension led to vast series of body measurements being done in an attempt to identify a homosexual body type. Seventeen such studies were reviewed by Ellis.[24] He concluded, 'The main consistent findings seem to be not that homosexual males have feminine body-builds and lesbians have male body-builds, but that both male and female homosexuals have immature anatomies. This may mean that their physiologic immaturity makes it difficult for them to adjust to a regular heterosexual way of life.'

Homosexuality and sociobiology

The concern whether homosexuality is inherited or not is one example of the argument about genetic determinism. One of the debating points in sociobiology (which is, as we have seen, specifically concerned with genetic determinism) is homosexuality: if successful individual reproduction is the sole reason for the spread and persistence of particular traits, how can we explain the occurrence of large numbers of people primarily or exclusively attracted sexually to members of their own sex?

In *Sociobiology* Edward Wilson offered two suggestions:

1. Homosexuality may result from individuals being homozygous

(i.e. inheriting the same allele or gene from both parents), for a gene which in single dose (*i.e.* inherited from only one parent) results in the production of more children than average, through higher sex drive, greater immunity to childhood diseases or some such mechanism. Such a mechanism is responsible for the high frequencies of the often fatal haemolytic disease, sickle-cell anaemia, in areas where falciparum malaria is common; Julian Huxley suggested many years ago that schizophrenia might be maintained by a similar mechanism.

2. A more intriguing possibility is that homosexuality may be maintained by kin selection if close relatives of homosexuals have more children as a result of their condition:

> The homosexual members of primitive societies could have helped members of the same sex, either while hunting and gathering or in more domestic occupations at the dwelling sites. Freed from the special obligations of parental duties, they would have been in a position to operate with special efficiency in assisting close relatives. They might further have taken on the roles of seers, shamans, artists, and keepers of tribal knowledge. If the relatives – sisters, brothers, nieces, nephews, and others – were benefited by higher survival and reproduction rates, the genes these individuals shared with the homosexual specialists would have increased at the expense of alternative genes. Inevitably, some of these genes would have been those that predisposed individuals towards homosexuality. A minority of the population would consequently always have the potential for developing homophilic preferences.[25]

If either of these suggestions is true, one should find that close relatives of homosexuals have more children than average. There seems to be no evidence on this point. Weinrich[26] has claimed that homosexuals consistently perform better than heterosexuals on IQ tests, and that in preliterate societies they frequently take on priestly roles through which they acquire power and financial rewards, which in turn could benefit relatives. But both these characteristics could be related entirely to environmental conditions – and there is no need to indulge in these searches for explanations if homosexuality is *not* inherited.

The trouble with sociobiological models is that the underlying deterministic mechanisms that are necessary for their functioning are everywhere unknown in humans. It is no use explaining why genes for homosexuality might be common, if there are no genes for homosexuality. And, we have to accept that there is no unequivocal evidence that there are such things as homosexual genes.

If homosexuality is not inherited . . .

There are three possible non-genetic causes of homosexuality.

1. *Hormonal.* No consistent differences have been found between homosexuals and matched controls for hormonal levels (especially steroids).[27] A number of workers have claimed hormonal irregularities in homosexuals, but none of these has been confirmed when repeated. Nor has any lasting effect on their children of hormones administered to pregnant women been established. Girls born to women treated with testosterone during pregnancy seem to be more 'tomboyish' than normal, but they have no tendency to develop into homosexuals. Likewise, the sons of such women are no different from normal.

Animal studies (mainly on rats) show that large doses of hormones at certain stages of pre-natal development may produce males defective in their subsequent adult sexual behaviour. It is difficult to investigate the importance of short-term hormonal upsets in humans, but it is worth quoting in this context from the important review by Money and Ehrhardt:

> The concept of a prenatal hormonal component in the eventual differentiation of homosexuality is difficult to sustain because the phenomenon of obligative homosexuality, to say nothing of facultative homosexuality or bisexuality, is by no means uniform in its manifestations. The erotic preferences and activities, and the general everyday behaviour of one obligatively homosexual person (male or female) may differ as widely from that of another homosexual as the behaviour of an obligatively heterosexual woman differs from that of an obligatively heterosexual man.[28]

2. *Social.* There are many anecdotes about homosexual behaviour following particular experiences (such as boarding school, prison or the armed services; or after homosexual rape), but no pattern has emerged from these. Indeed, it is clear from the sexual histories of a wide range of people that homosexuality may occur transitorily

wherever single sex communities occur, but that its persistence in individuals must depend on some additional factor in the history or make-up of the persons concerned.

3. *Psychodynamic*. Finally we come to a group of explanations that imply that homosexuality develops as a result of a defect or deficit in family (or other) relationships. There are several converging lines of evidence that support the importance of such factors.

Male homosexuals often have elderly mothers. This has been interpreted as indicating a chromosomal mutation in determination but, as we have seen, no chromosomal anomalies have been found in homosexuals. Its significance is more likely to arise from possible strains in the family relationships in such cases. Numerous workers have reported that male homosexuals have a particularly close relationship with their mother, and further analysis shows that the commonest pattern is when a son finds his father remote and unapproachable, combined with a particularly intimate relationship with an over-emotional mother. Such a pattern is found much more rarely among control series than in families identified through a homosexual male. (Knowledge about the families of homosexual females is much sparser.) Obligate homosexual males are almost always not fighters as boys. They remain low in the pecking order of their childhood groups. In contrast, homosexual females are likely to have competed for dominance as a child, and to have been weak in maternal play interests.

A developing child needs a model with which to identify. For a male, fear of women begins if he has difficulty in breaking his childhood ties with his mother. For a girl, adulthood begins when other women become competitors, not models. Anthony Storr defines homosexuality as 'a form of emotional immaturity which is dependent upon a failure to become identified with adult membership of one's own sex'. Elizabeth Moberly[29] has extended this. Agreeing that homosexuals have a deficit with parents of the same sex, she argues that:

> As a consequence, needs for love, dependency, and identification that are normally met through attachment to the parent of the same sex remain unmet. At the same time, there is a reparative drive towards the fulfilling of unmet needs, *i.e.* the homosexual

condition involves both a state of incomplete growth (as has been traditionally assumed) *and* a drive towards the completion of the developmental process. To evaluate the homosexual condition we should turn not to guidelines for adult sexuality, but to considerations of pre-adult development.

The homosexual condition

No consistent metabolic or proven genetic differences have been found between homosexuals and heterosexuals, and it seems safe to conclude therefore that there is no such thing as a person who will inevitably become a homosexual; homosexuality is the product of imperfect, incomplete interactions during developing sexuality. In terms of our general theme, the occurrence of homosexuals is most probably not primarily a result of genetic diversity (even though it is theoretically possible that there may be people who have innate difficulties in relationships with one sex or the other), but of the complex interactions of genes and environment that forge every adult. There is probably no such person as one who has no possibility of developing except as a heterosexual.

But having said that, there are very many homosexuals in the community who are desperately lonely, and who feel unfulfilled however much they identify with other homosexuals. (There are, of course, also lonely and unfulfilled heterosexuals, but the reasons for this are different.) Some manage to change their orientation. Masters and Johnson[30] report a failure to 'reorientate' in fully only 20 out of 155 obligate (Kinsey Grade 6) homosexuals, using techniques designed to affect close relationships. Pattison and Pattison[31] describe changes to heterosexuality in eight out of eleven exclusive male homosexuals following commitment to a pentecostal church fellowship, and review many other cases in the medical literature, emphasising 'the importance of ideology, expectation, and behavioural experience in producing change'.

Probably the answer to homosexuality and to homosexuals is to stop arguing about whether 'gay is good' or 'gay is bad', and to concentrate instead on the problem of what gives rise to the homosexual condition. To quote Elizabeth Moberly again:

> It is sometimes said that homosexuality is 'against the will of God'. Apart from noting that the traditional prohibition refers

only to homosexual *acts*, there is a further point to be made here. If homosexuality involves a certain deficit in normal growth, then it is surely these deficits – and not the attempt to meet them – that is 'against the will of God'. The perfect will of God for human growth is checked whenever a child is orphaned. However, although being an orphan is in this sense 'against the will of God', one does not therefore seek to punish an orphan for being an orphan. The analogy may prove to be an especially close one: if homosexuality involves certain deficits in the parent-child relationship, the homosexual may perhaps be regarded as a type of psychological orphan. In such a situation, however, does not seeking the will of God imply doing all that one can to make good the deficits involved?

In Chapter 2 we saw that a proper knowledge about the nature of life changes the questions we have to ask about artificial insemination, *in vitro* fertilisation, abortion, and so on; with homosexuality (and, for that matter, other sexual variations) we must seek the right questions to ask, and make our moral judgments in the light of the answers to those questions. And we must remember also that the grace of God is an integral part of the ability to ask the right questions and to find a proper basis for moral judgments. Many can testify to the value of Christian fellowship and community in helping them face themselves. The principles behind this are developed by David Atkinson in Chapter 3.

Pornography

Another example of sexual ethics shows the confusions produced in and by liberals who are caught between commercial pressure and what they see as moral persecution by traditionalists. Pornography has an assortment of apologists, ranging from psychiatrists, who see it as providing therapy for bored marriage partners; through sociologists, who believe that police time could be better used than by prosecuting pornographers, and advocates of homosexual and women's rights, who regard minority discrimination as immoral; to radicals who find their efforts for change hampered by the conservative structure of a society based on the nuclear family.[32] The response to this torrent of ideological commitment tends to be that, at worst, pornography does no harm and should therefore be permitted, despite 'the tastelessness and depressing awfulness of pornography generally . . . the total emptiness of almost all the material. . . . Most pornography is trash: ugly, shallow and obvious'.[33] For example, a Presidential Commission in the USA reported in 1970 that 'extensive empirical evidence, both by the Commission and others, provide no evidence that exposure to or use of explicitly sexual material plays a significant role in the causation of social or individual harms such as crime, delinquency, sexual or non-sexual deviancy or severe emotional disturbances'. (They came to this conclusion despite some of the evidence they themselves published. For example, one study showed that the reactions of people exposed to pornography was 'the strongest predictor of sexual deviance'.)

In Britain, a Home Office Report, *On Obscenity and Film Censorship* (the Williams Report) reviewed three lines of evidence (anecdotal, experimental, demographic) in an attempt to identify harm produced by pornography, and concluded that it causes no harm. However, its evaluation was defective on three grounds:

1. It used a legal test, that the causation of harm should lie 'beyond reasonable doubt'. In fact there are indications from all strands of evidence that pornography *can* cause harm. The correct procedure would have been to deal with the cumulative probability of harm.

2. Harm is likely to be quantitative not qualitative. For example, mild erotic material reduces aggression, but more sexually arousing material increases it; aggressive cues turn off inhibition to sexual behaviour.[34] It is easy to argue futilely about the interpretation of population statistics relating to pornography. For example, the oft-quoted liberalisation of pornography laws in Denmark has not produced a decrease in sex crimes as it is often asserted. Rape cases in both the UK and Denmark have approximately trebled in the past twenty years, despite different changes in attitudes and law. The sort of inane generalisation that often appears is typified by a statement emanating from the American Commission: 'One million adults in the USA have had personal experience of obtaining relief from a sexual problem by means of exposure to pornography.' This statement is an extrapolation from a survey of 2,468 people in which

0.6 per cent fifteen individuals said they had received help in sex problems from pornography; this is one in 150, or one million in a population of 150 million. However, the same survey found that 2 per cent reported a 'decline in' their personal morals, and 7 per cent in their respect for females. Perhaps more significantly, 47 per cent of men and 51 per cent of women thought that pornography might stimulate some people to commit rape.

3. The main false assumption in the Williams Committee review was that all people are alike in their response to stimuli. Despite the perennial hopes of liberal humanists, it is manifestly untrue that everyone reacts in the same way to pornography. The Committee opined that in the cases of the 'Moors murderers' (who stripped and gagged a ten-year-old girl, photographed her in pornographic poses, and made a sixteen-minute tape recording of her screams while torturing and killing her), and of the 'Cambridge rapist' (found guilty in 1975 of six rapes within a year), 'it would be extremely unsafe to conclude, even tentatively, that exposure to pornography was a cause of the offences committed'. They conclude, '*for those who are susceptible to them* [my italics], the stimuli are all around us'.[35]
But who is susceptible? Is it a few psychopaths, or is it a significant proportion of the population? The Committee:

> received some evidence that although exposure to deviant pornography might not induce a sexual taste in a person without a pre-existing bias in that direction, it might nevertheless bring to the surface a deviant ingredient in that person's character which he or she did not even know existed, or make it more difficult for people with deviant tastes to deal with that aspect of their personalities. . . . Where the balance lies as regards the control of this material is not easy to judge.

Others find it much easier. For example, Pamela Hansford Johnson[36] recalls that the Moors murderers were students of the Marquis de Sade, 'I cannot help but wonder whether, by making all books available to all men, we do not pay too high a price, if that price should be the death of one small child by torture.' And at the trial of the Cambridge rapist it was said that he was a connoisseur of sex films, which he watched and supplied to his neighbours

– 'What had been nothing more than a private obsession became a public menace. He would watch a film, then go out and rape.'[37] The Williams Committee themselves recorded: 'While we have been preparing this report, the IRA have planted a bomb in a manner modelled on an incident in a television crime series; a 12-year-old boy has been reported as shooting himself in Detroit while playing Russian roulette after seeing [the film] *The Deer Hunter;* and an 8-year-old girl has jumped from a second-floor landing in Barcelona after telling her playmates she was *Superman*. . . . The net would have to be cast very wide to prevent actual events from being influenced undesirably by what people see.'[38]

The Williams Committee was specifically considering the regulation and possible restriction of books and films. My concern is much more general: it is abundantly clear that different people react differently to the same stimulus. And, more particularly, some individuals may harm themselves or others when they read a book or see a film which is merely titillating or simply boring to others.

It would be presumptuous to claim to be able to identify those who react antisocially. A proportion of them are psychopaths, who present a diagnostic problem to professional psychiatrists. But a substantial group (and perhaps the majority) are the lonely and unfulfilled, who seek artificial thrills because they have not managed to make normal relationships; in Anthony Storr's language, they are emotionally immature or stunted. Such people illustrate the variety of humankind, but they are also examples of behavioural incompleteness rather than "normal" adult variants.

The Williams Committee devised a set of recommendations on liberalising the sale of pornography and the showing of sex films, on the grounds that pornography causes no harm. In its formal response to the government, the Board of Social Responsibility of the Church of England concluded:

> The Committee has failed to establish that pornography does no harm. This does not mean that we have preconceptions or evidence of our own on this point, although we affirm the statement that pornography is an assault on human values and represents a moral offence by its mere existence, regardless of what it leads to. Our concern is that the Recommendations of the Committee are based on a false premise, and should not be acted

on until the hazards of pornography to individuals and society, to the mature as well as to the young and weak, are better known.

John Milton argued in *Areopagitica* (1644) that true virtue is only possible in the context of trial and temptation: 'He that can apprehend and consider vice with all her baits and seeming pleasures, and yet abstain, and yet distinguish, and yet prefer that which is truly better, he is the true warfaring Christian. I cannot praise a fugitive and cloistered virtue, unexercised and unbreathed, that never sallies out and sees her adversary, but slinks out of the race.' Without dissenting from this in principle, we must also remember Christ's words, 'Temptations to sin are sure to come; but woe to him by whom they come! It would be better for him if a millstone were hung round his neck and he were cast into the sea, than that he should cause one of these little ones to sin' (Luke 17. 1, 2) (RSV). While it may be true that pornography does no harm to mature adults, there are many who are adult in years but socially and emotionally immature. For these, and for the young, we must be terribly cautious in permitting unrestricted availability of pornographic material.

Sexual diversity or sexual normality?

So far in this chapter we have been concerned to discuss the factors that act to produce variation in individual sexuality. It is only fair, therefore, to ask if there is such a thing as sexual normality; in other words, can we define permissible limits to sexual behaviour, outside of which sexual expression can fairly be described as abnormal and hence potentially immoral?

In considering this question, it is dangerous to rely simply on a supposed Christian tradition, since much of Western Christendom has leaned far too heavily on the Greek idea that the body is either evil or irrelevant, and that the only serious problem is the care of the soul or spirit. As we saw in Chapter 2, we are created as man-soul, and it is illegitimate to separate body from soul. As Calvin pointed out, we are at one and the same time apart from nature and a part of nature. Moreover, attempts from Christian bodies to correct this situation have tended merely to muddy the situation.[39] It is all very well to decry the action of Origen in having himself castrated, of Clement who told women that they should be ashamed at the very thought of being women, or Augustine who called women 'a temple built over a sewer'. But is there a more positive or scriptural attitude that reflects reality rather than a philosophical abstraction or religious sanctimoniousness?

Despite centuries of Church influence (including that of the Reformers), actual sexual mores in this country have probably changed little throughout historical times. For example, Laslett has assembled the percentages of baptisms following less than nine months of marriage of their parents in seven diverse parishes:

1550	31.6
1600	21.3
1650	17.6
1700	24.6
1750	35.2
1800	38.5

The pill and legalised abortion have changed such statistics, but they have not diminished the likelihood of pre- or extramarital sex (rather the reverse). And never mind heterosexuality, anyone with even a rudimentary acquaintance with Shakespeare or the Restoration playwrights knows how familiar they were with homosexuality, transvestism, voyeurism, and other sexual byplays. It is easy to condemn such behaviour, and point to the perils of promiscuity (for example, an epidemic of a previously rare cancer is spreading from practising American homosexuals), but responding to the sex urge is easy to justify to oneself and not easily assuaged.

I believe the best way to summarise the situation is to examine our attitude to sex from the negative and from the positive point of views.

A negative view of sex: quantification

Sexual acts can, in principle, be recognised and counted. I may covet, laze, denigrate my colleagues, and do all manner of other sinful acts roundly criticised by Christ,[40] but I may be able to delude myself and others that I am living a holy and upright life. Once I indulge in adultery, fornication, homosexuality, pornography, or any other sexually related behaviour, my actions can, as it were, be counted and scored against me.

Stephen Jay Gould[41] has exposed the terrible excesses that emerge once we start measuring characteristics that we believe have some deep significance for character. He shows how women, 'lower classes', and blacks (and other races) have been quantitatively 'proved' to be less intelligent than white men by measurements of head bumps, brain size, or IQ; and that virtually all the supposed differences stem from the presuppositions of the investigators. This does not mean that there are not differences between the mean intelligence of different races, etc.; what Gould was concerned to point out was that the differences within a group are larger than those between groups, and that it is impossible to predict the performance of an individual from knowing the mean of his or her group. Gould himself regarded his book as a tract against biological determinism: once a trait can be measured or counted, it must exist (so it is claimed) and must therefore have a cause; on the same argument in the context of sexual behaviour, once a person offends, he is guilty of a recognisable sin and therefore someone to be condemned.

The 'liberal' response to sexual deviation is either deterministic ('he/she couldn't help it') or situational ('in the circumstances, it was excusable'). These two explanations ought to be recognisable as inadequate in the light of the twin half-truths of determinism and reductionism that have recurred again and again in this book:

1. It is *not* true to claim that we are powerless to modify any behaviour. No behaviour is irrevocably determined by genes, family background, social circumstance, or anything else.
2. *All* our behaviours have to be seen outside the immediate context that elicited them. If I find myself alone with a beautiful and sensuous girl, when we have both drunk too much alcohol, my behaviour needs considerable will power (and grace) to control it; but I also need to explain why I found myself in that situation. It is futile to claim that the overriding motive for any behaviour should be love, because love *per se* is powerless to discriminate between the immediate and the wider situation.

A positive view of sex: mature relationships

A complex trait may vary considerably in its manifestation, depending on the strength and timing of all the factors (genetical and environmental) that contribute to it. Sexual disposition depends on interactions between genes (determining maleness or femaleness, and governing hormone secretion) and the establishment of relationships at different stages of growth. If these go wrong, we may finish up 'incomplete' and, to a varying extent, incapable of normal sexual response. In other words, we behave sexually as children even when we are adult in years. Now, there is nothing wrong in children behaving as children, but there is a good deal wrong about adults continuing to behave like children.

One of the main aims of the London Lectures is to take a fresh look at traditional Christian doctrines and attitudes in the light of contemporary Christian attitudes and knowledge. In Chapter 2 we saw that new knowledge from molecular biology enables us to open the 'black box' we call life, and thus rephrase the questions we have to ask about the nature of life. In this chapter, we have seen that sex is neither a simple male–female dichotomy nor a male–female continuum, but is the maturing of a series of relationships with parents, family and society.

And it is through this understanding of sex that we can best develop our attitudes to variations in the expression of sex. It is perhaps no accident that Paul had most to say about sex in his letters to the Corinthians, and that it is in them also that he is explicitly outspoken about immaturity (1 Cor. 3.1–7; 2 Cor. 6.12, 13) – 'When I was a child, I spoke like a child, I thought like a child, I reasoned like a child; when I became a man, I gave up childish ways' (1 Cor. 13.11) (RSV). Although we can certainly define and refer to 'sexual abnormality', perhaps we should be more ready to talk about 'sexual immaturity', and treat those who cannot enter into full sexual relationships both within and outside families with the blend of care and discipline that we use towards children. Behaviour that is tolerated and expected in children is irritating and often dangerous in adults.

Conclusion: Free to differ?

Gay Talese has chronicled how a relatively small group of people have changed attitudes to sex in the USA since 1945.[42] In this period an apparently orthodox society has been replaced by one in which virtually every form of sexual activity is common, and where the philosophy of the Puritans and pioneers has been replaced by Hugh Hefner's *Playboy*, Alex Comfort's sex manuals, gay rightists, transient 'marriages', and the like. Of course, this is only one side of the coin, but there is no question that sexual licence has been widely legitimised in the name of freedom. Talese's story is a depressing one. He gives many case histories (including his own), which show clearly that the pursuit of pleasure is only temporarily satisfying, and virtually all the people we meet in Talese's book end in depression, or else revert to traditionally orthodox behaviour.

Are there any constraints on our sexual behaviour? Should there be any? I have suggested that much of what we commonly call sexual deviation is really immaturity. But what about straight heterosexuality? Are we free to copulate at will, subject only to the necessity of providing reasonably stable homes for any children? Or what? Christians have had much to say on this, sometimes trivially but often helpfully.[43]

In the first place, it is worth noting that it is false to claim that the 'natural' breeding system of humans is promiscuity within a group, like the other great apes, for the simple reason that every ape species has a different breeding and sexual structure. Male gorillas, for example, copulate only once or twice every two or three years. For what it is worth, Desmond Morris has argued that firm bonding between individual pairs has been an essential element in human evolution.

However, the most important arguments for human monogamy are:

1. Although we are in one sense able to indulge in any behaviour we like, in another sense we indulge at our peril. If there is really a pair-bond between my wife and I, we clearly endanger it if either of us commits adultery. And breaking (or stressing) the bond is likely to produce psychological symptoms and affect my relationships with all my circle, never mind my spouse. This is, of course, a variant of the traditional 'natural law' argument, but it is as well to recognise that sexual profligacy may be costly. We can measure the physical consequences of sex, but not as yet the psychological (and spiritual) correlates.

2. The Christian accepts by faith that he is a man-soul, and not just an animal. The Bible is explicit in its teaching that men and

women should join in 'one flesh'. I have commented in Chapter 2 that I interpret this phrase to mean much more than physical coupling. Quite apart from the scriptural teaching about divorce, it seems absolutely clear that monogamy is God's pattern for his children, although he gives special grace to some to remain single or childless, so that they can perform particular tasks for him.

3. Marriage is under strain from external propaganda (the apologists for women's rights, pornography, 'sexual freedom' generally), but also from internal pressures: for too long it has been assumed that marriage is about sex. This was explicitly taught by the Church. For example, the Book of Common Prayer says that marriage was primarily 'ordained for the procreation of children', and secondly 'to avoid fornication; that such persons as have not the gift of continency might marry, and keep themselves undefiled members of Christ's body'. Only thirdly are we told that 'it was ordained for the mutual society, help and comfort that the one ought to have of the other'. Yet God originally made marriage for companionship (Gen. 2.18, 24; Matt. 19.5), and the separation of sex from reproduction through contraception and some of the techniques described in Chapter 2, may not be as important or as destructive as is often made out. Unfortunately many marriage partners seem to have great difficulty in communicating with one another: they are happy in bed and in a crowd, but otherwise rarely talk to one another. If a couple do not communicate, neither the social nor the spiritual bonds between them can develop properly. Although sex is obviously a part of marriage, it ought to be a secondary part of it. The argument that the separation of sex from reproduction weakens marriage is a poor one and in practice has little effect on a union that develops and deepens as time passes.

When one talks about sex, one is wide open to accusations of insensitivity, incomprehension, and many other faults. All of us are sex experts, at least about ourselves. In the space of a single chapter, it is almost impossible not to oversimplify and select. Perhaps with regard to sex more than anything else we need to pray with understanding for ourselves and others: 'O God, give us strength to change those things that we can change, the patience to accept those that we cannot change, and the wisdom to know the difference, for Jesus Christ's sake.'

Notes

1. Cf. John Money and Anke Ehrhardt, *Man and Woman, Boy and Girl* (Johns Hopkins University Press, 1972).
2. A. Kinsey, W. B. Pomeroy and C. E. Martin, *Sexual Behaviour in the Human Male* (Saunders, 1948).
3. Peter Singer, *The Expanding Circle* (Oxford University Press, 1981), p. 149.
4. Charles Darwin, *The Descent of Man,* (Macmillan 1871).
5. W.D. Hamilton in *Journal of Theoretical Biology,* vol. 7 (1964), pp. 1–32.
6. Edward Wilson, *Sociobiology: The New Synthesis* (Harvard University Press, 1975).
7. Edward Wilson, *On Human Nature* (Harvard University Press, 1978).
8. See Michael Ruse, *Sociobiology, Sense or Nonsense* (Reidel, 1979).
9. Richard Dawkins, *The Selfish Gene* (Oxford University Press, 1976) (expanded in *The Extended Phenotype* (Freeman, 1982),) pp. 3 and 215.
10. T. H. Huxley, *An apologetic Irenicon,* Fortnightly review No. 52, 1 November 1892, p. 569.
11. Kinsey, 1948.
12. 1953.
13. M. Schofield (*Promiscuity,* Gollanz, 1973 p. 151): ‘It might be better if we recognised that every day hundreds of people have intercourse because they are sexually attracted to each other, and for that reason alone; they are not in love and they do not want to live together for the rest of their lives.’
14. Anthony Storr, *Sexual Deviation* (Pelican, Harmondsworth, 1964), p. 12.
15. Comparisons between societies can be very difficult to interpret. Anthropological studies are often quoted to claim that the Christian insistence on (say) fidelity in marriage is extreme, artificial, and distorting to relationship. For example, in a world-wide survey of sexual habits, C. S. Ford and F. A. Beach (Yale Cross-cultural Survey, 1952) found that ‘formal restriction to single mateship’ prevailed in only 16 per cent of 185 societies examined, and less than one-third of these wholly disapproved of pre- and extra-marital liaisons. However, in his much-quoted work on the Trobriand Islanders of north-west Melanesia, where ‘infantile and playful sensualities grade into serious permanent relations which precede marriage, with special bachelor’s houses provided for couples if they wanted amorous privacy for an hour or two’, B. A. Malinowski specifically warned that in no way

could the Trobriand situation be regarded as 'a homily for our own failings'. Thus he noted that homosexuality and adult masturbation was rare and regarded with contempt and derision and as a grossly inferior substitute for heterosexual relationships. Margaret Mead had similar reservations about generalising (or moralising) from the sexual patterns she found in Samoa.

16. Cf. Peter Coleman, *Christian Attitudes to Homosexuality* (SPCK, London, 1980).
17. Derrick Sherwin Bailey, *Homosexuality and the Western Christian Tradition* (Longmans, Green, London, 1955). Critically reviewed by Richard Lovelace, *Homosexuality and the Church* (Revell, 1978) and by Michael Green, David Holloway and David Watson, *The Church and Homosexuality* (Hodder & Stoughton, London, 1980).
18. Church Information Office, 1982.
19. Cf. David Field, *The Homosexual Way – A Christian Option?* (Grove Ethics Booklet, 1976); David Atkinson, *Homosexuals in the Christian Fellowship* (Latimer House, London, 1979).
20. For a valuable summary of pastoral aspects, see Roger Moss, *Christians and Homosexuality* (Paternoster Press, Exeter, 1977).
21. 1936, p. 175.
22. *American Journal of Human Genetics*, vol. 4, p. 136 (1952).
23. L. C. Heston and J. Shields, *Archives General Psychiatry*, vol. 18, p. 149 (1968).
24. *Advances in Sex Research*, 1963, p. 177.
25. Wilson, *On Human Nature*, Bantam edition p. 150.
26. Weinrich, *Journal Homosexuality*, vol. 3, p. 275 (1978).
27. Cf. R. C. Friedman and A. G. Frantz, *Hormones and Behaviour*, vol. 9, p. 19 (1977).
28. Money and Ehrhart, *Man and Woman, Boy and Girl* (Johns Hopkins University Press, p. 233, 1972).
29. Elizabeth Moberly in *Theology* (May 1980).
30. W. H. Masters and V. E. Johnson, *Homosexuality in Perspective* (Little, Brown, Boston, 1979).
31. Pattison and Pattison, *American Journal of Psychiatry*, vol. 137, p. 1554 (1980).
32. For example, Wilhelm Reich has written, 'As the conditions of life in large cities deteriorate and the explosive tensions of an increasingly dehumanised affluent society magnify, there is political advantage to be gained by channelling rebellion into personal forms which can be manipulated commercially, and by increasing social provision of various forms of 'sexual relaxation therapy' of the type once limited to the night club or pornographic book shop'.

33. *Home Office Report of the Committee on Obscenity and Film Censorship*, cmnd 7772, 1979, a committee chaired by Lord Longford. pp. 56, 95, 96. The Longford Report defined pornography as 'that which exploits and dehumanises sex, so that human beings are treated as things, and women in particular as sex objects'. Kenneth Tynan regarded it differently: 'It has a simple and localized purpose, to produce an erection. And the more skilfully the better. Contrary to popular myth, it takes craft and devotion to produce ideal results. These usually take the form of solo masturbation.' (*The Observer Review* 28 Jan. 1968, p. 27).
34. J. H. Court, *Pornography: A Christian Critique* (Paternoster Press, Exeter, 1980).
35. Williams Committee, p. 64.
36. Pamela Hansford Johnson, *On Iniquity* (Macmillan, London, 1967).
37. *Cambridge Evening News*, 3rd October, 1975.
38. Williams Committee, p. 65.
39. For example, Alistair Heron (ed.), *Towards a Quaker View of Sex* (Friends Home Service Committee, 1963); *Sex and Morality* (British Council of Churches, 1966); Basil and Rachel Moss, *Humanity and Sexuality* (Church Informtion Office, 1978). A recent Anglican report on *Homosexual Relationships* (CIO, 1979) was described as 'bewildering' by the *Sunday Telegraph*, and as 'baffling' by the *New Statesman*. A Methodist Report was only accepted by the Methodist Conference when a major section was added pointing out that the radicalism of the original conclusions did not follow from the known facts, and that a more traditional explanation was more faithful to Scripture.
40. Cf. John Stott, *Christian Counter-Culture* (IVP, Leicester, 1978).
41. Stephen Jay Gould, *The Mismeasure of Man* (Norton, London, 1981).
42. Gay Talese, *Thy Neighbour's Wife* (Collins, London, 1980).
43. A valuable discussion is that of L. Smedes, *Sex in the Real World* (Lion, Tring, Herts, 1979).

6: Conscience

David Atkinson

Our third case study is about conscience, that seemingly ever-present yet elusive part of our human person which has to do with our capacity to be moral beings. We are to explore some of the contributions of 'nature' and 'nurture' to the development of what we experience as moral sense, and to try to understand this experience within the framework of Christian theology.

We have been concentrating in this book on the varieties of human behaviour, and on the various factors that determine how we in fact behave. In particular we have looked at environmental conditioning, our genetic inheritance and the gracious activity of God towards us and in us. We have also thought about the freedoms we experience within the limits of these determinants: our freedom to choose, our freedom to be different from one another, our freedom to change within ourselves. We are responsible, it has been argued, within these limits, for the choices we make. To be 'responsible' within limits includes living responsibly 'before God' within the limits of our bodies, of our backgrounds, of our temperaments, of our religious awareness, of our sexual disposition and so on. We have suggested that though all of us have a real freedom of choice, we cannot all exercise that freedom before God without God's grace for us and in us. Grace sets our experience of the world on a new footing (changing, for instance, the presuppositions on which our science is based, and setting boundaries of responsibility in research); it also gives the Christian a personal moral resource, which can push back some of the limits of nature and nurture, and so expand the parameters of our personal freedom. The gracious power of Christ can set us free from some aspects of prior conditioning. It can also create in us new attitudes towards those parts of us that we cannot change.

Does grace, then, override the rich variety of differences between us and make us 'spiritual clones'? Not at all. God's grace reaches us in the full variety of our differences, and uses them as vehicles for his different workings, his different gifts. We are to rejoice in our variety, recognise one another's gifts and temperaments, and realise that because of our different genes, and different backgrounds, we will not all feel the same, think the same, believe the same or behave the same. We will not all have the same religious experiences, nor will we all be prone to the same sexual inclinations. So I will try to understand that if you are different from me, that does not necessarily mean that I am right and you are wrong! All this we have discussed in the previous chapters.

But are we really able to talk about 'right' and 'wrong'? In all this rich variety, are there some courses of action that are right and others that are wrong? Are there some things that are good and others bad? And if so, how are we to tell? If it was right for some sixth-century Irish Christians to stand up to their necks in water and think of holiness, would it be right for us to do that? Or is it perhaps not a matter of right and wrong, but of cultural conditioning and personal preference? But what about someone with a sexual disposition different from ours? Would it be right or wrong for him or her to act sexually in a way that we might believe to be 'wrong'? Is this also a matter of cultural conditioning and personal preference? From where do we get our sense of right and wrong, good and bad? What authority does such a sense hold? These are some of the questions that we will have in mind as we turn now in more detail to a consideration of *conscience*.

We will first look at what we mean by 'moral sense'; on this topic I have three propositions to discuss. Then we will consider how developmental psychology may shed some light on the growth of moral sense within us. We will try to assess this discussion from the perspective of Christian theology. Finally, after a brief glance at the way the idea of conscience features in the Bible, I want to examine the relationship between Christian conscience and Christian freedom. Our aim throughout is restricted by the general title of this book, *Free to be Different*, with a concentration on factors relevant to personal behaviour.

Moral sense: three propositions

Here, then, are three preliminary propositions.

First, *virtually all human beings have a moral sense.* It is a good question to ask whether this sense is inborn or not; in one sense the answer is yes, in another sense no. As Gordon Allport has written,

'Quite clearly, specific ideas of what is right and wrong are not innate. Cultures are too variable. Individuals are too variable. To honour the sabbath day is not an injunction to trouble the Hawaiian conscience. Nor is the sin the Hawaiian feels at eating standing on his feet a source of concern to the Christian conscience. The cultural relativity of conscience is marked.' But having said that, he goes on: 'At the same time, it is equally evident that the *capacity* for conscience exists in nearly every person. In the course of his social living, the individual is bound to form a conscience. Only in the very exceptional cases of what modern science sometimes calls psychopathy do feelings of right and wrong seem absent.'[1] Allport quotes a Babylonian prayer of 4,000 years ago, revealing a very sensitive conscience.

> O my God, my transgressions are very great, very great my sins. I transgress and know it not. I wander on wrong paths and know it not. I am silent and in tears and none takes me by the hand. My God who knowest the unknown, be merciful. In the midst of the stormy waters come to my assistance, take me by the hand.

John Macquarrie in his book *In Search of Humanity*[2] has a chapter on 'Conscience' in which he refers to the claim of classical Chinese philosophy: 'Every one has within him the principle of right, what we call *Tao*, the road along which we ought to walk.' in *The Abolition of Man*,[3] C. S. Lewis picks up this idea of the *Tao* and suggests how many different cultures and thinkers, despite all the cultural diversity of what in detail is held to be right or wrong, propose very similar moral precepts as fundamental guides to what is good and what is right (for example in the areas of truth-telling, respect for human life, sexual behaviour).

My second proposition is that *morality is unique.* That is to say, moral terms cannot be reduced to non-moral terms. By 'moral terms' I mean words like 'ought', 'good', 'evil', 'right', 'wrong', when they are used in the context of moral obligation. A number of moral philosophers wish to translate moral terms into something else. Might it be said, for example, that 'good' really means 'pleasurable', or perhaps that it really means 'higher up the evolutionary scale'? But, as H. P. Owen argues,[4] this sort of reductionism fails to observe two important distinctions:

1. There is first a distinction to be made between description and evaluation. A psychologist might be able to describe our sense of right and wrong in terms of conditioned reflexes, for instance, or (if we were to take a Freudian model) in terms of the demands of the superego. But to *describe* something in psychological terms is not to *evaluate* it in moral terms. The sentence 'He really *wants* to get rid of his mother-in-law' is different from the sentence 'He really *ought* to get rid of his mother-in-law'. However we describe our actions, we are still left with the altogether different task of evaluating them.

2. The other distinction this reductionism fails to observe, is that between 'ought' and 'is'. There is much discussion about this distinction, but the only point I wish to make here is the impossibility of deriving obligations from so-called empirical 'facts' alone. Peter Green[5] tells of a Marxist shop steward who believed that all supposedly moral beliefs were socially and historically conditioned. According to this view, moral laws, so called, are nothing but the reflection of the existing economic system, and will change with that system. Now of course our culture and social structures do greatly influence who we are and how we behave. But we also have to account for the fact that an Amos or a Jesus can *confront* the social values of their day and not merely reflect them. It is possible to believe that society is wrong, judged by some standard outside society. To return to the shop steward, Peter Green asks: 'Suppose you find your wife going out with another man, and excusing herself by saying that the economic situation in which the husband is placed did not allow her to enjoy herself, would you say that she was right?' Description is not the same as evaluation. 'Ought' does not follow from what is empirically the case. Are there not – as the *Tao* might indicate – some universal moral norms that cross all social and cultural differences?

This sort of reductionsim is not confined to psychological or sociological determinism. There is a growing viewpoint in the biological sciences, and particularly in the field of sociobiology, that morality is really the strong imprinting on our nature of certain behaviour patterns that have a built-in survival value. To do what is right might then be described in terms of 'fitting in with the process and direction of evolution'. But despite the difficulty of trying to derive moral beliefs from evolutionary – or indeed any scientific – theory, and at the same time using such beliefs as the criterion by which to live and thus to influence the scientific processes, it is simply not clear that all moral rules are really aimed at biological survival. Was Jesus' moral courage in the face of the cross really only fear of infringing some biological behaviour pattern? And is it true that we believe ourselves to be called on merely to conform to 'nature'? Sometimes – in medicine for example – we believe it right to confront, attack and heal what seems from the point of view of biology to be 'natural'. That sense of 'right' does not derive from biology.

My third preliminary point is that *there is an objectivity about moral values*. There are many people, Hamlet among them, who say 'there is nothing either good or bad, but thinking makes it so'.[6] Goodness, in other words is 'in the eye of the beholder'. But this does not correspond with the way we in fact treat moral judgment as the basis for rational disagreements. It is one thing to say 'I like tea, you hate tea'. I accept that and do not try to convert you. But if you say 'I hate Jews', and you try to exterminate them, I feel a sense of outrage; I believe you are doing something evil; I believe that there are reasons for saying that you are wrong. Morality, in other words, can give rise to rational disagreement; it is not simply a matter of taste and temperament. There is a difference between believing passionately in Nazism, believing passionately in neighbour-love, and believing passionately in avoiding all the cracks on the pavement, in case the bears come out. Moral values are not merely the expression of subjective feelings. If I say 'Fred is good' I intend to say something *about Fred* and not merely about my pro-attitude towards him. When we are confronted with a holy person, we believe there is something of objective goodness in his character. Furthermore, some good acts can be done in secret when there is no one there to have a pro-attitude towards them. We could surely say they are objectively good acts, even before they can be praised.

There is another dimension to this 'objectivity' of moral values:

when we feel what we call the pricking of our conscience, is it not *a feeling of being confronted* by moral obligation from without?

These three propositions are only, of course, hinting at issues that form the substance of a great deal of writing in moral philosophy.[7] I am leaving them as suggestions that, from our experience of the way we do in fact think and behave, a moral sense is virtually *universal*, moral values are *irreducible* and there is an *objectivity* about them.

We turn now from these suggestions to a theological framework; in particular to see what help the Bible may give in understanding these sorts of experiences.

A biblical perspective

In the primeval history of early Genesis we find this interesting trio of verses: 'Of the tree of the knowledge of good and evil you shall not eat'; 'God knows that when you eat of it your eyes will be opened, and you will be like God, knowing good and evil'; 'Behold, the man has become like one of us, knowing good and evil' (Gen. 2.17; 3.5; 3.22)(RSV).

It is an exegetical question whether the author is intending to convey that through his fall into sin man now has experiential knowledge of evil in contrast to good, or whether the sense is rather: 'your sense of good and evil will now haunt you as an inescapable ideal from which you have now fallen'. Either way, in this author's mind, from the very beginnings human beings have had an awareness of good and evil. Then the story of God's covenant with Noah is made as a covenant with 'every living creature' (Gen. 9.8–17): it tells of a more ancient covenant than that made more particularly with Abraham. Later in the Old Testament writings all human life is held in moral covenant with the Creator. There are further hints that all men, whether believers in Yahweh or not, have a capacity for moral awareness and moral choice. When Amos denounces the peoples around, for instance, does he not implicitly appeal to some standard of justice of which his hearers are aware and by which they stand condemned?

Is there not the same assumption in the New Testament? Peter urges his Christian readers to 'Maintain good conduct among the Gentiles, so that in case they speak against you as wrongdoers, they may see your good deeds and glorify God' (1 Pet. 2.12). In Peter's mind there is in the Gentiles a capacity for moral judgment that will lead them to recognise that what the law tells believers is good. Similarly, in Paul's view, the agent of government referred to in Romans 13.1–6 is a 'servant of God for good'; this service must depend on the capacity to distinguish between good and evil.

Jesus asks the multitudes 'Why do you not judge for yourselves what is right?' In some of the parables, accepted human standards of good and evil are used to support teaching about the character of God. Sometimes the link is explicit: 'If you then, who are evil, know how to give good gifts to your children, how much more will your Father who is in heaven?' (Matt. 7.11)(RSV). In Jesus' discussion about divorce as reported in Matthew and Mark, he appeals not to the law, but to the pattern of creation for his view of the intended permanence of marriage.

There seems underlying much of the New Testament a belief that certain fundamental standards of goodness and evil were 'given' in creation: there is a 'Creator's pattern' for human life.[8] There is one paragraph in which the structure of the created universe is used by Jesus to disclose something of our moral sense: 'Love your enemies and pray for those who persecute you, so that you may be sons of your Father who is in heaven . . . for he makes his sun rise on the evil and on the good, and sends rain on the just and on the unjust' (Matt. 5.44f.)(RSV). C.H. Dodd comments on this, 'His sayings imply an order of creation containing within it the fundamental traits of God's design from human conduct.'[9]

Is not this sort of thinking in the mind of Paul when he writes the two classic passages that seem to indicate what some wish to call a 'natural law'? They are Romans 1.19–21 and 2.14–15. The first says that ever since the creation of the world what can be known about God has been made plain in his creation. In the second, he says that, 'When the Gentiles who have not the law do by nature what the law requires, they are a law to themselves . . . they show that what the law requires is *written on their hearts,* while their conscience also bears witness and their conflicting thoughts accuse or perhaps excuse them . . .' 'Written on the heart' means engraved in the depths of human personality.

Is not Paul's meaning that there is something in the moral sense of all human beings that matches the revealed law of God? Calvin put it the other way round: that the universal fact of conscience is a strong pointer to the existence of a conscience-creating God. But what both Paul and Calvin seem to link together is that it is by virtue of our creation as men and women by God that there is within us a capacity for distinguishing right from wrong.

Conscience and psychological development

We turn now to the accounts of conscience that are offered by the various psychological disciplines. I shall restrict myself to brief comment on one or two authors.

Within the field of developmental psychology, the psychodynamic approach stemming from Freud, but modified considerably in different ways since, is influential in some clinical and therapeutic practice, though less so in academic experimental psychology. One of the most widely read recent writers in this school is Eric Erikson, who moved from Freud's concentration on infantile sexuality to a much broader analysis of the development of a sense of personal identity. Erikson's concern – like Freud's – is with emotional development. He describes the processes of maturation in terms of specific crisis phases, each of which has a particular emotional component, the predominant feelings of which are associated with the relationship between the growing child and its parents.[10] In his own valuable discussion of the origin of conscience Jack Dominian comments on Erikson's approach in these words:

> Since the majority of children remain with their parents throughout childhood, the conspicuous traits of the parents will become the features that are widespread in the personality of the growing person.
>
> Such a description [as Erikson's] emphasises the influence of the environment, in the form of the parents. But clearly this is only one of the determining factors. The make-up of the child, its genetic inheritance, will be the other influential factor making it more or less resistant to an adverse influence, more or less co-operative with any advantageous one.
>
> All growth proceeds in this interaction between the inherited resources and the environmental influences. This explains how

children may grow up to be markedly different from each other even though they are brought up by the same parents.[11]

According to Erikson, it is the negotiation of the phases, especially of the early years (of what he calls 'basic trust versus mistrust'; of 'autonomy versus shame'; of 'initiative versus guilt'), that significantly affects a growing child's capacity for moral awareness. In healthy growth there is a progression from what we may call an 'imposed' or external morality – which is an 'internalising' of values authoritatively given by others – towards the maturity in which a person makes moral judgments of his own.

Sometimes, according to this approach, the context of growth is such that there may be unsatisfactory development, and so a stunting of conscience before it can develop into a mature moral sense. This may give rise to what some theologians used to call an 'over-scrupulous conscience'.

Here is a sad story of a girl with whom I was at college. She came from a very exclusive Christian group, and had been taught that it was always necessary for women to cover their heads when they prayed. To my amazement she always carried a handkerchief in her bag to put on her head when she said 'grace' before meals. And when she did this once in the college refectory before a cup of coffee, I said 'Why do you cover your head to say grace before a cup of coffee?' She replied – and this is the sadness – 'Just in case'. Hers was an 'over-scrupulous conscience': what would her father have said if he had caught her with her head uncovered?

Such an over-scrupulous conscience feels the promptings of conscience only as a threatening condemning judge, inducing painful feelings of guilt. In the more mature person, conscience operates also in a forward-looking way: not only as judge, but as guide.

Recall Launcelot Gobbo, the servant of Shylock the rich Jew in the *Merchant of Venice*. We may not regard him as particularly mature, but he illustrates conscience as both judge and guide. Gobbo is caught between the voice of the devil tempting him to run away from Shylock, and the voice of his conscience:

> Certainly my conscience will serve me to run from this Jew, my master. The fiend is at mine elbow, and tempts me, saying to me, *Gobbo, Launcelot Gobbo, good Launcelot, or good Gobbo, or*

> *good Launcelot Gobbo, use your legs, take the start, run away.* My conscience says: *No; take heed, honest Launcelot; take heed, honest Gobbo; or* as aforesaid, *honest Launcelot Gobbo; do not run; scorn running with thy heels.* Well, the most courageous fiend bids me pack: *Via!* says the fiend; *away!* says the fiend, *for the heavens; rouse up a brave mind*, says the fiend, *and run.* Well, my conscience, hanging about the neck of my heart, says very wisely to me – *My honest friend, Launcelot, being an honest man's son*, or rather an honest woman's son . . . my conscience says, *Launcelot, budge not. Budge*, says the fiend. *Budge not* says my conscience. Conscience, say I, you counsel well; fiend, say I, you counsel well: to be ruled by my conscience, I should stay with the Jew, my master, who (God bless the mark!) is a kind of devil; and, to run away from the Jew, I should be ruled by the fiend, who, saving your reverence, is the devil himself.[12]

Here is conscience both as 'judge' – the sense of condemnation Gobbo will feel in infringing it – and conscience as 'guide', 'hanging about the neck of his heart'.

By contrast with the psychodynamic concentration on feelings, other psychologists are concerned primarily with intellectual development. From Piaget's classic work on the development of moral judgment,[13] there has been considerable modification in theory,[14] one of the most significant contributors to which has been L. Kohlberg. Kohlberg developed Piaget's view that cognitive development proceeds through various stages and levels. Dominian summarises much of the work associated with this sort of approach to the development of moral judgment in terms of a progression 'from prudential, to the authoritarian, social and personal'.[15] As with theories of emotional development, there is considerable disagreement within psychology as to the experimental basis for many of these conclusions, but several writers[16] believe that we need some model of personal development that considers both cognitive and affective aspects of personality.

Together with theories of personal development, there are other schools of psychologists who concentrate from an experimental basis more on the mechanisms of learning, and have developed theories of the ways in which human behaviour patterns are actually acquired, maintained and changed, through the formation of 'stimulus-response bonds'.

This is not the place for discussion of psychological theories in any detail, but I have mentioned this to remind ourselves that conscience as an aspect of personhood has both a thinking and a feeling aspect, and therefore the processes of emotional and cognitive development as well as mechanisms of learning are likely to be crucial factors in the development of conscience. Furthermore, education of conscience will necessarily be different for different ages: for the child, for the adolescent, for the more mature adult.

As we grow towards maturity we can learn gradually not only to accept but also to question. We become aware of moral values not only through the voice of our parents, but also through other voices external to them and to us. Our more mature conscience can learn to discriminate between what of our inherited conditioning in moral awareness we will keep and what we will cast off. We can grow towards 'internalising' other values, derived from the other objects towards which our 'heart' is directed.

The capacity for moral judgment, in other words, can grow as we grow, with the right stimulation and education. For some people, growth towards moral maturity can be stunted and stifled through a hostile environment. Some of us are too *afraid* to outgrow our parents' morality – 'outgrow' not in the sense of disagreeing with them, though it may be that, but in the sense of making morality our own.

The psychoanalyst Harry Guntrip writes:

> One of the greatest blessings a child can have is parents whose character and conduct exemplify definite values, but who are sufficiently mature to know that they do not possess a monopoly of wisdom, who do not get over-anxious or angry if disagreed with, and who rejoice to see the child learning to think for himself.[17]

The narrow line of good parenting, therefore, has both to enable the growing person to take over what is valuable from the past, and to avoid the tyranny of authoritarianism that creates a punishing 'internalised parent voice'. The latter most likely leads either to cramped people with an over-scrupulous conscience, unable to grow, or to rebels who throw over everything and so tragically do not take anything of value from the past.

How are we to assess this discussion from a theological perspective? We recall how conscience has both a 'thinking' and a 'feeling' aspect. Some Christians have emphasised the one, some the other. Both are important. As Bishop Butler expressed it in his cryptic way, conscience may be understood as 'a sentiment of the understanding, or a perception of the heart; or, which seems the truth, as including both'.[18] In mature life, conscience is both judge and guide. It comes as judgment or guidance from without, but it is felt within. We internalise some external moral standard or goal and make it our own.

Our conscience, therefore, is part of our deepest essential selves: of what in Chapter 3 we called the 'heart'. And in biblical language, the 'heart' is where the voice of God is heard, where the moral sense is focused. The conscience, to pick up Gobbo's phrase, 'hangs about the neck of the heart'.

Bonhoeffer put it this way:

> Conscience comes from a depth which lies beyond a man's own will and reason, and it makes itself heard as the call of human existence to unity with itself. Conscience comes as an indictment of the loss of this unity and as a warning against the loss of one's self. Primarily it is directed not towards a particular kind of doing, but towards a particular mode of being.[19]

It can never be advisable, therefore, to act against one's conscience; to do so would be to act against what makes for the inner unity of heart, and so to act against one's very self.

The question that needs to be raised at this point, however, is: around which values is our maturing conscience to be integrated? Around which values is this 'unity' of existence to be found? As we grow towards maturity, responding not only to parental voices but to others, internalising other standards and making them our own, is our conscience necessarily open to what is objectively the good? In other words, was Pinnochio right: 'Always let your conscience be your guide'?

Here we are again at the fundamental question of the nature of man, and from where we derive our values of what makes for man's best good. From a Christian perspective we need to say both that all of us – whether Christian or not – can grow towards a degree of psychological maturity and individuality, and also that our conscience may none the less be integrated around a value system that is ultimately destructive or evil. When the National Socialist of Nazi Germany said 'My conscience is Adolf Hitler', he was seeking a unity of his own self beyond himself, but how disastrously misplaced we would judge that to have been.

If we are creatures of God, what makes for maturity, integration and fulfilled individuality will involve a congruence of our own internal sense of moral value with the external moral norm of the character of God from whom we derive and on whom we are dependent.

In an objective sense, therefore, Pinnochio would be right, were this not a fallen world. But in fact our conscience is open to signals not only from God, but also (as we have said) from our parents, our peers, from the social structures around, from Adolf Hitler or other public figures. Some of these voices may be in line with the voice of God, and some not. Our conscience only leads us rightly if it is integrated around an objectively good value system.

For the Christian, this external norm of good is the character of God revealed to us in Christ. If our conscience were always to be an infallible guide to what is good, we would always need to be able to say 'We have the mind of Christ'. Our integration point would then be not ourselves, nor our parents, nor Hitler, but Christ himself. And even were we to say 'the moral norm is love' (which it is), we would – because of our fallen nature – need some guiding principles to guide us in loving, some external norms by which to distinguish true love for neighbour from sinful self-indulgence.

To quote Bonhoeffer again:

> When Christ, true God and true man, has become the point of unity of my existence, conscience will indeed still formally be the call of my actual being to unity with myself, but this unity . . . must be realised in fellowship with Jesus Christ. Natural conscience, no matter how strict and rigorous it may be, is now seen to be the most ungodly self-justification, and it is overcome by the conscience which is set free in Jesus Christ and which summons me to unity with myself in Jesus Christ.[20]

Bonhoeffer then even says, in conscious opposition to the National

Socialists of Nazi Germany where he lived: 'Jesus Christ has become my conscience'.[21]

Let us remind ourselves at this point of the work of grace through death and resurrection to which an earlier chapter referred, transposing our being into a different key, setting our 'heart' in a new direction. The Christian, we said, is at a point of tension. If we were fully in the 'new creation' in every part of our being, we would truly have the mind of Christ, our conscience would be the internalised values of the character of God. But we are still open to other signals that we may have to call in question, and that need to be measured by what we know of God's character and will. This is the slow hard practice of Christian love and obedience to which the writer to the Hebrews refers: 'those who have their faculties trained by practice to distinguish good from evil' (Heb 5.14) (RSV).

With all this in mind, let us turn back now to the biblical records, and examine rather more closely some allusions to conscience both as judge and as guide.

The Old Testament does not really have a word for 'conscience', but the notion is there. In Psalm 38.3–5, the writer speaks of a heavy sense of inner guilt. He is weighed down with wrong, believing that he feels what God feels. Here is the judge at work. In another psalm (32.8–9), we read of a strong sense of divine guidance: a voice within, not that we are dragged along by God like a mule without understanding, but that within there can be a sense of divine direction. The example of David, however, serves as a reminder that what we believe in our heart is not necessarily the truth: we may be led astray. His conscience seemed clear enough after his affair with Uriah and Bathsheba. It was only when Nathan confronted him with his wrong that he realised that his good feelings were complacency and not a good conscience (2 Sam. 12).

In the New Testament, we have already noted the strand in Paul's thinking that speaks of a capacity in all men for moral judgment, and indeed a deep inner sense of some fundamental aspects of what is good and what evil. But Paul also writes a great deal about 'walking in darkness' and about the heart being led astray. In 1 Timothy 4.1–5 we read of the possibility of the conscience being 'seared' through demonic influence. This may mean 'branded' by Satan, or cauterised and so made insensible to the distinction between good and evil, like the pagans in Ephesians 4.19 who are 'dead to all feeling'. The point is that Christians can be led astray into foolish scrupulousness about things that God created to be enjoyed (food and marriage, for example). Then in Titus 1.15 we are told that the conscience can be corrupted by coming to believe that pure things are really impure. Conscience can build up habits of thinking on false pretences. The New Testament epistles seem to indicate, over against Pinnochio, that conscience cannot always be trusted.

Yet, while conscience gives no absolute certainty of good in an objective sense, and we need some external norm against which to measure it, on the other hand conscience is spoken of as of the very highest importance. 'For our boast is this,' says Paul, 'the testimony of our conscience that we have behaved in the world, and still more toward you, with holiness and godly sincerity, not by earthly wisdom but by the grace of God' (2 Cor. 1.12) (RSV).

A good conscience is of great importance because, as Calvin put it, before God a good conscience is 'nothing but inward integrity of heart'. In this sense we read of the 'fulfilment of the law' as 'love from a clear conscience and a sincere faith' (1 Tim. 1.5), and later of how certain people had made 'shipwreck' of their faith because they had forsaken a good conscience.

By way of an interim conclusion, therefore, let us take stock of our discussion so far.

We conclude that conscience is an inner moral sense, an aspect of our feeling and thinking, which makes us aware of obligation to do what is good and right. Our capacity to feel and to think like this grows through childhood, and – if it is not stunted – can become a mature and self-directing capacity. However, the *direction* of the conscience needs to be kept in line with an objective external moral norm, the revealed character of God in Christ if it is to serve as a capacity for hearing God's words of judgment and guidance. It is important for us to follow our conscience and not to act against it, for it is part of the heart of our personal being. It is equally important for us to educate our conscience by God's moral character, and to learn by practice to internalise the mind of Christ. The Christian is in this process of growth in a double sense: of psychological development towards the maturity of an adult conscience, and of spiritual growth of the direction of the conscience towards God, and towards the mind of Christ.

Conscience and Christian freedom

We turn now to an examination of some of the links to be drawn between what we have said about conscience, and the Christian understanding of 'freedom' as the New Testament discloses it.

Freedom from 'the condemnation of the law'
Some Christians are prone to hear the voice of God as an authoritarian external moral demand; perhaps they replace the condemning voice of an 'internalised parent' with what is taken to be the condemning voice of a threatening God. Outside the grace of Christ, God's moral character does show up our distance from God, and the New Testament does speak of the law of God in terms of its condemnation. But the gospel of grace is that in Christ we are set free from this condemning sense of law. We still fall short of God's character of holy love, but we are set free in our conscience from the condemnation of that failure. Too many of us say that we believe in the freedom of the gospel, but we still live under the threat of the law. We need the Holy Spirit's aid in making the grace of Christ real in our consciences, and so make sense in experience of Paul's affirmation that 'there is now no condemnation' (Rom. 8.1). For some of us, our consciences are so trained in habits of guilty feelings that we may need particular pastoral help, or therapeutic help, as a vehicle for the liberty of the Spirit.

This is not to say that freedom from the *condemnation* of the law is freedom from the law itself. On the contrary, Paul himself speaks of being 'under the law of Christ' (1 Cor. 9.21), and John writes, 'this is the love of God, that we keep his commandments' (1 John 5.3) (RSV). But this 'law' is no external moral code imposed from without; it is the law 'written on the heart' by the Spirit within (cf. Jer. 31.33; Ezek. 36.26f.).

Freedom from others' norms
A good conscience – what Calvin called 'inward integrity of heart' – liberates us also from the critical judgment of other people, and indeed from the critical judgment of ourselves. 'I thank God whom I serve with a clear conscience' writes Paul (2 Tim. 1.3) (RSV). He has no sense here of critical self-accusation. The Christian is called to realistic self-assessment, to accepting himself as accepted in

Christ; his conscience in fellowship with Christ can be at peace. Paul also guarded himself against the hostile criticism of other Christians. 'With me,' he wrote 'it is a very small thing that I should be judged by you or by any human court. I do not even judge myself. I am not aware of anything against myself, but I am not thereby acquitted. It is the Lord who judges me' (1 Cor. 4.3) (RSV).

On the one hand, Paul built a great deal on a clear conscience; on the other hand, he knew that what mattered was God's view of him. If our minds are primarily concerned with God's view of us, and God's acceptance of us in Christ, we will be helped to cope with the critical voices even of fellow Christians who misunderstand or misrepresent us, and with habits of self-accusation we may have developed.

Freedom in 'things indifferent'

Some Christians 'major on minors'; they stress as being of crucial importance to their faith matters that others regard as within the area of legitimate disagreement. Let me quote again from Calvin:

> The third part of Christian freedom is this: regarding outward things that are of themselves 'indifferent', we are not bound before God by any religious obligations preventing us from sometimes using them and other times not using them, indifferently. And the knowledge of this freedom is very necessary for us, for if it is lacking, our consciences will have no repose and there will be no end to superstitions. . . .
>
> When consciences once ensnare themselves, they enter a long and inextricable maze not easy to get out of. If a man begins to doubt whether he may use linen for sheets, shirts, handkerchiefs and napkins, he will afterwards be uncertain also about hemp; finally doubt will arise even over tow. For he will turn over in his mind whether he can sup without napkins, or go without a handkerchief. If a man should consider daintier food unlawful, in the end he will not be at peace with God when he eats black bread. . . . If he boggles at sweet wine, he will not with clear conscience drink even flat wine, and finally he will not dare touch water, if sweeter and cleaner than other water. To sum up, he will come to the point of considering it wrong to step upon a straw across his path.[22]

But what, we may properly ask, are the 'essentials', and what are the 'things indifferent'? Is the prohibition of alcohol for Communion essential or 'indifferent'? Is the use of some forms of contraceptive 'against the law of God' or 'indifferent'? And what of the many other areas in which – as this book has been stressing – we are different from each other?

This is not the place for a full discussion of these issues, but only to point to the importance of giving each other freedom of conscience in matters that are not 'essential'. I have two comments to offer:

1. The 'fundamentals' are 'fundamentals of the gospel'. There was much discussion about *adiaphora* ('things indifferent') in contrast to the 'fundamentals' in the seventeenth century, and it was, I think rightly, on the criterion of the essential themes of the gospel that the criteria for discrimination were based.

Daniel Waterland was an Anglican theologian at the close of the seventeenth century. He became Archdeacon of Middlesex, and one of his charges to the Middlesex clergy at his Easter visitation was called 'A Discourse of Fundamentals'.[23] Without going into full detail, it is of interest to summarise the sorts of issues he regarded as 'essential' to the faith, fundamentals of the gospel. A 'fundamental doctrine' he said, is such a doctrine as is in strict sense 'of the essence of Christianity, without which the whole building and superstructure must fall'. He spoke of Christianity as a covenant between man and God, whose fundamentals are therefore the following:

- the deity and perfection of God, the Creator and Provider;
- the freedom of man's will sufficient for him responsibly to enter into covenant;
- the charter of the foundation: the sacred oracles of Holy Writ;
- the mediator of the covenant: the divinity and humanity of Jesus Christ and his atoning death;
- the conditions of the covenant: repentance, faith and a godly life;
- the means to enable the performance: the means of grace, the sacraments of the Church, the gift of the Holy Spirit;
- the sanctions to bind the covenant and to secure obedience: the doctrines of the Resurrection and the final judgment.

There is much else implied here also, but it points to the way in which one divine thought the question should be approached.

2. My second comment concerns the Church. Although on the one hand we are not to sell our consciences to others, on the other hand we are not on our own. Christian faith is the faith of the people of God, and the learning, discriminating, judging process of training our faculties by practice to distinguish good from evil (cf. Heb. 5.14) takes place within the community of faith. It is 'with all the saints' (Eph. 3.18) that we are to comprehend something of the love of God. The community thus acts as a check on our individuality. Conscience is heard as the private voice within the person but it is to be formed within the community of faith. The community of faith is the place where we must learn to discriminate between the will of God given for all time, and the ways the expression of that will have been refracted through the structures of our fallen world and sinful Church, and have been culturally conditioned in their expression by different Christians at different times.

Freedom in relation to past and present

We are not bound by our past. The grace of God, we argued earlier, creates the resurrection of new life, new attitudes, new possibilities. Conscience can be a repository of past mistakes and failures. We need to learn in our consciences that principle of death and resurrection to which a previous chapter referred. God's forgiveness can enable us to break with the condemnation and guilt of past failure. Forgiveness is also something to do with breaking down false idealisations in the present. We can set ourselves unrealistic goals, or have these imposed on us by others, and when we fail our consciences feel bad. If we can learn a realistic self-assessment, we can learn to forgive ourselves when we let ourselves down, and our consciences can be free.[24]

Limits to the freedom of my conscience

We have spoken in earlier chapters of the limits placed on us by our genes and our environment, and that grace can sometimes enable us to expand the parameters of personal freedom; sometimes help us in coping with what we cannot change. We have also spoken of the limits placed on us, as a goal and an ideal, of living in a spiritual and moral universe as beings dependent on God.

There are further limits placed upon our consciences: we are limited by the fact that others have consciences too. As one who is called to love my neighbour, I need to remember that neighbour love includes respect for his conscience.

At the heart of a discussion about conscience in which some believers with scruples were having problems about eating meat that had been offered to idols, Paul wrote to the stronger ones who had rightly outgrown such scruples: 'Let no one seek his own good, but the good of his neighbour' (1 Cor. 10.24). Especially if we are not persuaded that the issue between us belongs to the 'fundamentals of the faith', we are to take great care not to override the conscience of our brother.

There are wide varieties of differences between us in many things. Some of us have had the opportunity to grow up in a favourable environment. Some of us have had to struggle very hard all the way. For some of us faith has come easily; for others, our weak faith barely seems to hold on. Paul recognises such differences. On many things he encourages us to be free to be different. He urges his readers to express their differences in harmony. Perhaps his words of exhortation in Roman 14 and 15 form a fitting conclusion to this chapter – especially for those of us who think ourselves 'strong' in the faith, and prone on that basis to be critical of others:

> As for the man who is weak in faith, welcome him . . . for God has welcomed him. . . . Let every one be fully convinced in his own mind. . . . If we live, we live to the Lord . . . each of us shall give account of himself to God. . . . Decide never to put a stumbling block or hindrance in the way of a brother . . . walk in love . . . pursue what makes for peace and for mutual upbuilding. . . . We who are strong ought to bear with the failings of the weak, and not to please ourselves; let each of us please his neighbour for his good, to edify him . . . whatever was written in former days was written for our instruction, that by steadfastness and by the encouragement of the scriptures we might have hope. May the God of steadfastness and encouragement grant you to live in such harmony with one another, in accord with Christ

Jesus, that together you may with one voice glorify the God and Father of our Lord Jesus Christ (Rom. 14.1–15.6) (RSV).

Notes

1. Gordon Allport, *The Individual and His Religion* (Macmillan, London, 1950), pp. 98f.
2. John Macquarrie, *In Search of Humanity* (SCM, London, 1982).
3. C.S. Lewis, *The Abolition of Man* (Oxford University Press, 1943; Collins (Fount), 1978).
4. H. P. Owen, *The Moral Argument for Christian Theism* (Allen & Unwin, London, 1965).
5. Peter Green, *The Problem of Right Conduct* (Longmans, Green, London, 1932).
6. Shakespeare's *Hamlet*, act II, scene 2.
7. They are explored in a little more detail in Vernon White's *Honest to Goodness* (Grove Ethics Booklet, 1981), no. 40, which includes a good bibliography.
8. Cf. here B. Kaye and G. Wenham, *Law, Morality and the Bible* (IVP, Leicester, 1978), part II, ch. 1.
9. C. H. Dodd, in *Theology* (May 1946).
10. Cf. E. Erikson, *Childhood and Society*, rev. edn. (Granada, St Albans, 1977).
11. Jack Dominian, *Authority* (Darton, Longman & Todd, London, 1976), ch. 4, p. 30 (my square brackets).
12. Shakespeare's *Merchant of Venice*, act II, scene 2.
13. Jean Piaget, *The Moral Judgment of the Child* (English trans. Routledge & Kegan Paul, London, 1932; Penguin, 1977).
14. Cf. William Kay, *Moral Development* (Allen & Unwin, London, 1972).
15. Dominian, *Authority*, op. cit., p. 42.
16. For example, Dominian, and R. S. Peters, *Moral Development and Moral Education* (Allen & Unwin, London, 1981).
17. Harry Guntrip, *Psychology for Ministers* 2nd edn. (Independent Press, 1953), p. 313.
18. Bishop Butler, *Dissertation Upon the Nature of Virtue* (first published 1736; A. Bell & Sons, 1953).
19. D. Bonhoeffer, *Ethics* (trans. of 6th German edn, SCM, London, 1955, 1978), p. 211.
20. Ibid., p.212.
21. Ibid., p.212.
22. John Calvin, *Institutes*, III.19.7.

23. Daniel Waterland, *Waterlands Works* (Oxford University Press, 1843), Vol. 5.
24. Cf. David Atkinson, 'Forgiveness', *Third Way* (October 1982).

Epilogue

Malcolm Jeeves, R. J. Berry and David Atkinson

To be 'free to be different' implies the freedom to change one's beliefs and behaviour. But are we really free to do so? That is the question which has preoccupied us throughout this book.

We began by asking how far we are determined by either genetic or environmental factors. We saw that viewpoints differ. Some believe that the evidence currently available is insufficient to prove that the brain is a physically determinate system; others accept that such determinacy is a good, working assumption, but add that freedom of choice and action are not thereby eliminated. As for our social environment, it evidently shapes and constrains our behaviour. In fact, all of us are aware that the sort of people we are, the things we say and do, and our hopes and fears, are to a great extent the result of a complex mixture of our genetic make-up, early upbringing, education and social environment. The concern of this book, however, is not with the underlying academic debate about determinism, but with other more practical and pressing questions. How far are we free to change ourselves and our future? And how will our answer to this question affect our attitude towards ourselves and other people?

Another question follows. How should we view the limits to our freedom? Are we prisoners of our genetic and environmental background? Or is our background rather a personal challenge to overcome or transcend? Or again, are our limits fixed bounds which we attempt to overstep at our peril? And if we *are* free to be different, how different should we want to be? After all, in one sense all Christians should be alike. The Bible reveals a number of traits which should characterize every mature Christian. Jesus himself summarized them, for example, in the Beatitudes, and so did his apostle Paul in his list of 'the fruit of the Spirit'. Nevertheless, it is also made plain in Scripture that God gives us different natural talents and spiritual gifts, different callings and experiences. We are thus faced with a paradox. On the one hand, we are all summoned to become like Christ, the perfect human being. On the other, we are called to discern and do his particular will for each of us, e.g. in marriage or celibacy, in service at home or overseas, as a doctor, pastor, home-maker, teacher, administrator, industrialist or whatever. We are free to be like Christ, and we become more truly free the more we resemble him. We are also free to be different from one another, according to Christ's gifts and callings.

In answer to the question 'are we prisoners of our genes?', we gave the unequivocal answer that 'there is no automatic association between genes and the physical or behavioural trait that finally emerges'. Our genetic make-up *per se* is not all-determining. Rather the person resulting from our genes reflects our personal history from pre-natal environment through childhood to adulthood and maturity. And *we* are in large measure responsible for our personal history.

Factors which determine behaviour do not begin at birth. The environment in which the human embryo develops can significantly affect later growth. So can nutritional deprivation in the newborn. Yet we should not acquiesce in the current fashion which over-emphasizes the importance of the first few years of life for subsequent development. The whole of our human development is important. Even in later life personal change following a good or bad experience is possible. In addition, as we have seen, our behaviour is affected not only by external pressures, whether physical or social, but also by our own internal convictions about our freedom to change. A balanced view of these influences from within and without will help us to be more equitable in our evaluation of our own and other people's behaviour. Our tendency is to blame the environment for our failures and take the credit for our successes. At the same time, we tend to attribute total responsibility to others for their beliefs and actions, while lacking the sympathy to acknowledge the factors which have helped to make them the sort of people they are. The truth is that all of us are responsible within limits.

As Christians, however, we have something further to add. We need to set our thinking about 'nature' and 'nurture' within the wider context of 'grace'. The grace of God is his unconditional kindness, calling human beings into relationship with himself. Grace gives us a new freedom both from the determining effects of our inheritance and environment, and in biblical terms from the paralysing powers of sin, guilt, fear and death. Grace neither replaces our nature, nor is simply added to it, but transforms it through a continual process of 'death' and 'resurrection', with a view to perfecting, not abolishing it. In consequence, our new life in Christ enjoys with our previous life both continuity and discontinuity. We are still human beings, who 'eat and drink, marry and are given in marriage, laugh and cry, stand under authorities and within orders' (Helmut Thielicke), and, we added, we are to some extent determined by the genetic base of our personhood and the conditioning effects of our cultural environments. Nevertheless, none of these things either explains or enslaves us. For in Christ, as Paul wrote, we are 'a new creation' (2 Cor. 5:17). God's grace has changed us. Not that grace has made us spiritual clones. For God deals with each of us as the individual person we are. But grace can overcome the handicaps both of nature (sometimes through healing, always by transforming our attitude to ourselves, our bodies and our infirmities) and of nurture (often through the healing power of real Christian fellowship).

How do these themes of nature, nurture and grace help us to understand our behaviour?

The 1982 London Lectures went beyond general conclusions about environmental and genetic determinants of behaviour to consider the three case studies of religion, sex and conscience – topics which generate much debate, and on which sides are readily taken and entrenched positions held.

Religious beliefs, experiences and behaviour vary widely. This variation is to some extent connected with personality traits, upbringing, age and social pressures. By thus identifying some of the psychological origins of religious profession and practice, however, we by no means explain them away. The truth or falsity of a person's beliefs – religious, political or scientific – is not to be judged by subjecting him to a psychological analysis, but rather by examining the evidence for his case. Indeed, unbelief has psychological roots as assuredly as belief.

The practice of the Christian religion has varied greatly from century to century and from place to place. In assessing it, however, we shall be wise not to concentrate on superficial differences due to changing culture, but on Jesus Christ, whom we believe to be God in the flesh and the Saviour of the world. For he does not change, and the inspired biblical witness to him is the yardstick by which to measure the authenticity of every expression of Christianity.

Our second case study was concerned with sexual determination and sexual behaviour, and with the connections between them. The available evidence seems to indicate that sex is neither a simple male/female dichotomy, nor a continuum of male/female, but rather the maturing of a series of relationships with parents and family. We focussed on the question of homosexuality. We examined the causes of the homosexual orientation, and concluded that its origin is less genetic than psycho-dynamic, due perhaps to a deficit in same-sex parenting. We see both homosexual practices and family situations which may sometimes cause the homosexual orientation as contrary to God's will. But whatever our sexual orientation may be, to place our sexuality in a Christian context is to put it within the realm of God's grace, and to recognise that his grace is given us to change what can be changed, to accept patiently what cannot, and to distinguish between these two.

Our final case study was of conscience, and so of the differing moral beliefs and attitudes of human beings. To what extent are these the product of nature and/or nurture? We affirmed that almost every human being possesses an in-built moral sense. We went on to acknowledge, however, that our conscience, far from being created already stocked and programmed, reflects the mores in which we are brought up. If then our conscience is to fulfil its proper role in the Christian life, it must be informed by what God has revealed of his character and will. The Christian is always in a state of growth, – of psychological growth towards the maturity of an adult conscience, and of spiritual growth towards a conscience which discerns the will of God and the mind of Christ. God's grace can develop within us a 'strong' or well-educated conscience, which is free from false guilt, from excessive scrupulosity and from bondage to other people's norms.

The rich variety of differences between us is fully recognised in the Bible. In many things we are encouraged to be different from each other. Yet our differences need to be expressed in a spirit of tolerance and harmony. An appreciation of the factors which make us what we are should not only show us the possibilities and limits of our own freedom to change, but make us understanding towards others who are in the same position. Then, while we seek to live responsibly within the limits of our background, temperament, religious awareness and sexual disposition, we shall do so in the context of living responsibly before God and others.

But perhaps above all, we ought to regard our differences as a challenge and an opportunity – a challenge to become conformed to Jesus Christ rather than to the world, and an opportunity to contribute uniquely to God's purposes. For we are not automata, able to do nothing but react mechanically to our genes, our environment or even God's grace. We are personal beings created by God for himself. And just as we have a set of genes possessed by nobody else (unless we have an identical twin), so we have the possibility of serving God in a way that nobody else can. What is true of us is equally true of others. We rejoice in our variety. We affirm with enthusiasm the unique temperaments and gifts which God has given to others as well as to ourselves, all to be used in his service.

Moreover, what God has given us is not to be regarded as a static endowment. Our character can be refined. Our behaviour can change. Our convictions can mature. Our gifts can be cultivated. Scripture and Christian history are full of examples of the transforming grace of God. Grace gives us the personal moral resources both to push back some of the limits of nature and nurture and to come to terms with what cannot be changed. In both cases our personal freedom is thereby expanded. We are indeed free to be different, by God's grace and for his glory.